Perthshire

40 Town & Country Walks

The author and publisher have made every effort to ensure that the information in this publication is accurate, and accept no responsibility whatsoever for any loss, injury or inconvenience experienced by any person or persons whilst using this book.

published by
pocket mountains ltd
6 Church Wynd, Bo'ness EH51 0AN
pocketmountains.com

ISBN: 978-1-9070250-0-6

Printed in Poland

Introduction

Perthshire is at the very heart of Scotland, within easy reach of the cities of Glasgow and Edinburgh yet a world apart – offering a huge variety of scenery encompassing both Highland and Lowland landscapes. As well as the historic Fair City itself, Perthshire includes a number of attractive small towns – Pitlochry, Dunkeld, Crieff and Aberfeldy among them.

The mighty River Tay enjoys almost legendary status amongst salmon fishermen and it is just one of several fine rivers that carve their way through glens so richly wooded that the area has been branded 'Big Tree Country'. Remarkable trees include the Fortingall Yew – thought to be the oldest living organism in Europe – as well as the world's highest hedge, a contender for Britain's tallest tree and a surviving oak from Shakespeare's Birnam Wood. Above the trees are heather-clad hills and mountains – including lofty Ben Lawers and the graceful cone of Schiehallion, the Fairy Mountain.

A classic Perthshire image is that of the Highland castle, whether it be the dazzling white fairytale of Blair Castle, the dour fortress of Castle Menzies where Bonnie Prince Charlie stayed en route to Culloden or Scone Palace, where for many centuries the kings of Scotland were crowned on the Stone of Destiny. Other attractions include whisky distilleries (both Scotland's oldest and smallest are found here), historic gardens and golf courses, as well as events ranging from traditional Highland Games to Scotland's biggest music festival, T in the Park, and the Enchanted Forest, an extravaganza of music and lights.

This guide features 40 moderate walks in all parts of Perthshire and Kinross, including Killin near the head of Loch Tay, historically part of the region.

Safety and what to take

While some of the routes are waymarked, many others are not and the sketch maps accompanying them are intended as an aid to planning rather than navigation. It is recommended that you take – and know how to use – the relevant OS or Harvey map and compass.

Weather can be extreme on higher ground. The Ben Vrackie route, in particular, crosses high and exposed ground and, even at lower altitudes, the weather can change rapidly. It is always advisable to carry wind- and waterproof clothing and adequate warm layers to allow the walks to be completed safely if the weather does deteriorate. Most of the routes are suitable for families with children in good conditions and could be completed in stout walking shoes, but boots are recommended for the more exposed or rougher ground.

Access

Perth is served by railway lines from both Glasgow and Edinburgh, while a third line extends northwards through Perthshire en route to Inverness. Additionally, there are good bus services to most towns and villages throughout the region. Where a walk can be reached by public transport, it is indicated in the text. Timetables can be found in local tourist information centres and from Traveline Scotland.

The introduction of the Land Reform (Scotland) Act in 2003 gave walkers rights of access over most of Scotland away from residential buildings, but these rights entail responsibilities. Remember that much of the area is a working landscape, and always follow the Scottish Outdoor Access Code. In particular, keep dogs on tight leads during the spring and early summer and well away from sheep and lambs at all times. Deer stalking takes place on the hills from 1 July to 20 October, but this would not usually conflict with routes on lower ground as described here.

History

Perthshire has a very long and rich history. Although the Romans invaded this region under the leadership of Agricola, defeating the local Caledonian tribes at the Battle of Mons Graupius in 83AD, and later built a fort at Inchtuthil near Dunkeld, they were unable to subdue the tribesfolk for long and, after being subjected to a guerrilla campaign, retreated south. The best-known remains from this period are the crannogs, defensive loch dwellings, some of which date back to 5000BC. More than 20 such dwellings have been identified in Loch Tay alone, and there is an excellent reconstruction of one at the Crannog Centre near Kenmore.

Scone was the capital of the Kingdom of the Picts for many years while, further west, the Kingdom of the Gaels was centred on Dunadd in Argyll. Kenneth MacAlpin is traditionally claimed as the first King of Scotland and, according to legend, he brought the coronation stone, the Stone of Destiny, to Scone. Most modern historians believe it was his grandson Constantine, however, who truly united the two kingdoms when he overthrew a coup which had been carried out by a Gael, Giric. Constantine is thought to have defeated Giric at the hillfort of Dundurn above St Fillans. Whichever version of history is to be believed, Scone was the coronation place of the Scottish kings, and for several years it was also the seat of its parliament. When Edward I invaded Scotland he took the Stone of Destiny to Westminster, where, despite the Scots' eventual victory in the Wars of Independence, it remained in England until recent times.

The Glorious Revolution of 1688 saw the protestant William of Orange depose his uncle, the Catholic James II of England and VII of Scotland, to take the British throne. Many in northern Scotland were sympathetic to the exiled King and a series of uprisings in support of both James and his heirs wreaked havoc in the Highlands.

The first rising was led by John Graham who defeated the government forces at the Battle of Killiecrankie, just north of Pitlochry, in 1689, and was soon repressed. The next uprising was in 1715, led by the Earl of Mar in support of James Edward Stuart, the son of the deposed King. Within a fortnight of raising the standard near Braemar, Aberdeen, Montrose and Inverness had all fallen to the rebellion. The Earl of Mar himself occupied Perth with 5000 men. Mar was no military expert, though, and with his advance southwards blocked by fewer than 3000 government troops under the command of the Duke of Argyll from Blair Atholl, momentum was lost. Argyll received reinforcements before the eventual battle at Sheriffmuir, where both sides claimed victory but the Jacobites retreated to Perth. James Stuart briefly set up court at Scone, but eventually fled the country and his followers returned north.

In the aftermath of the rebellion, the government began an attempt to subdue the Highlands. Under General Wade, construction began on a series of forts and by 1830 he and his men had built a road from Dunkeld to Inverness, extending the existing route north from Perth. This was followed by a road connecting Crieff and the Dunkeld road via the Sma' Glen, creating a link with Stirling. The Tay was spanned by Wade's Bridge at Aberfeldy, the most expensive single structure on his entire road-building programme. Wade's efforts did not, however, prevent the second major uprising, led by Bonnie Prince Charlie in 1745. The Jacobites were eventually crushed at Culloden in 1746 and the Highlands repressed ruthlessly.

The clan system began to collapse as the remaining chiefs abandoned their role as guardian of their people and began instead to look for profits. The Industrial Revolution in the south was creating a massive demand for wool and the chiefs began to evict their tenants to make way for sheep. Perthshire did not escape the Highland Clearances entirely – with areas such as Glen Tilt and Glen Lednock largely emptied of people.

When the demand for wool declined, many estates turned to forestry. While the first commercial plantations were on Drummond Hill above Loch Tay, planted by Sir Duncan Campbell in the early 17th century, it was the Dukes of Atholl who began planting on a huge scale – around 27 million conifers in the 90 years to 1830.

Now, too, tourism began to take off, with deer-stalking, grouse-shooting and salmon-fishing the fashionable pastimes of Britain's elite and writers such as Robert Burns, William Wordsworth and Sir Walter Scott attracted to the area. Estate owners catered for such visitors by constructing follies, bridges and grottoes in places like the Hermitage near Dunkeld and the Falls of Acharn above Loch Tay. Rising incomes and improved transport slowly brought the region within the reach of the general public, and its popularity has continued to this day.

The handsome stone-built town of Pitlochry has been one of the most popular resorts in the Highlands ever since Queen Victoria visited more than 150 years ago. The town is perhaps best known for its Festival Theatre and for the salmon ladder beside the Faskally Dam, but it is the fine setting that draws visitors time and time again. The glens here are green, fertile and richly wooded, the mountains, rounded and beckoning, and the rivers truly magnificent.

To the north, the Pass of Killiecrankie, which is now bypassed by the A9, leads through ancient woodland to the quieter village of Blair Atholl with its celebrated

castle. The scenery here is more dramatic and Highland in character, with Glen Tilt stretching away as one of the most beautiful glens in all Scotland, accessible only on foot.

West of Pitlochry is Loch Tummel and the Queen's View. The landscape becomes progressively wilder and emptier on the approach to the lovely village of Kinloch Rannoch at the foot of Loch Rannoch. Looming above is the fairy mountain of Schiehallion, almost a perfect cone, before the road finally ends at the wilderness of Rannoch Station.

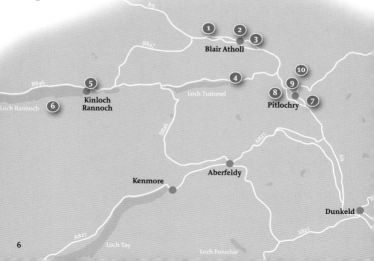

6

Pitlochry and North Perthshire

The Falls of Bruar

Distance 2.5km **Time** 1 hour 30
Terrain well-made path, steep sections
with sheer drops **Map** OS Explorer 386
Access bus (87) from Pitlochry

The series of cascades that make up the
Falls of Bruar have been attracting
visitors for more than 250 years. William
Wordsworth and Queen Victoria both
came here, as did Robert Burns in earlier
times. This short but steep loop climbs
upstream through pretty woodland with
various viewpoints and bridges before
returning down the opposite side.
Although the path is clear, take care with
children near the steep sides where there
are vertical drops into the ravine.

The walk begins beside the House of
Bruar shop and restaurant complex just
north of Blair Atholl. Boasting what are
possibly the poshest toilets in the

Highlands, the House of Bruar has built a
reputation for quality products, including
a mouthwatering selection of food
produced in the local area. From the car
park, skirt around the back of the building
before turning left to shadow the Bruar
Water. The path passes under the
Edinburgh-Inverness railway line and
through a gate to follow an obvious route
through the woods, with the river rushing
through a series of deep pools far below.

People began to visit the falls as road
construction opened up the area in the
1720s. On coming here, Robert Burns was
moved by the bare hillsides to write 'The
Humble Petition of Bruar Water' in which
he pleaded with the 4th Duke of Atholl to
clothe the barren slopes with 'lofty firs and
ashes cool'. After Burns' death, the Duke
began building the path network and
bridges as well as planting the first of the

◀ Falls from the Lower Bridge

pines. These original plantations, begun around 1796, were mostly felled to provide wood during the Second World War. Planting resumed after the war to provide the mixture of pine, birch, rowan, aspen and willow that can be enjoyed today.

The path ahead passes a flight of wooden steps, which climbs up to a viewpoint on the right. This overlooks the first of the falls, with a rock arch across the riverbed as foreground. Continuing upstream, you come to the Lower Bridge where to the left you'll see an arch – the remains of a 'viewing house'. The early tourists liked to frame their views with arches or grottoes, often hiding them until the last moment for dramatic effect. Viewing houses were built with narrow entrances to provide sudden 'surprise' views of waterfalls and ravines. Do not cross the Lower Bridge yet, but instead continue on the now steep uphill path on the near side. Further up, ignore the path which climbs to the left away from the river. Eventually, you reach the Upper Bridge, handsomely built to enable the early visitors to appreciate the falls. Its situation gives beautiful views downstream and out over the unfolding Perthshire countryside.

Cross the bridge and follow the path on a rising course for a short distance. To the left is another path to a picnic area with a great outlook over the Bruar Water. The walk continues on the path as it curves to the right through Scots pine and begins its descent towards the Lower Bridge, passing a number of good vantage points over the falls along the way. When you reach the Lower Bridge, cross the water to rejoin the outward route, turning left to head back to the start of the walk.

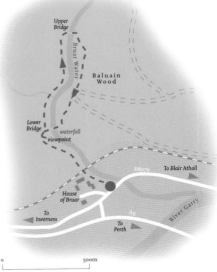

Glen Banvie and The Whim

Distance 6km **Time** 2 hours
Terrain clear, waymarked track, minor
road **Map** OS Explorer 386 **Access** bus (87)
or train from Pitlochry to Blair Atholl, a
short walk from the start

**Follow the Banvie Burn past stone
bridges and through a wooded glen to
visit the charming settlement of Old Blair
and the gothic arches of The Whim.**

The walk starts at the well-signed car
park near the Old Bridge of Tilt. From Blair
Atholl, follow the road north to Old Bridge
of Tilt and left through the village, then
cross the bridge to find the car park on the
left. This approach can also be made on
foot, which adds 3km to the round trip.

Leave the car park by the main entrance
and turn left along the road. Bear right at
the fork to follow the sloping road gently
uphill. Go straight ahead at the crossroads
onto a path, which passes a bungalow.

Keeping to the black arrows, fork left to
enter Banvie Woods. As elsewhere in the
Highlands, the Atholl Estate is battling
against the spread of the pervasive
rhododendron which, though planted
here as an exotic species in the 18th
century, has thrived to such an extent that
it poses a serious threat to biodiversity –
responding to hard pruning with equally
aggressive growth. Red squirrels can
sometimes be seen in the woods, but
you're more likely to hear them
scampering up and down the tree trunks.

Branch left to reach an old stone bridge
over the burn. Instead of crossing here,
continue on the track and bear left at the
next fork to reach upper Banvie Bridge.
During late summer, the open hillsides in
front of you are ablaze with purple heather
while in winter you may spot red deer

◀ The Whim

sheltering on the edges of the wood.

Cross the bridge to begin the walk back down the far side of the burn. Carry straight on where the gently rising track is joined by another from the right, then bear left at the next fork to pass the first bridge you encountered. Further on, you'll see a turn-off to the right, signposted for 'The Whim'. This is a stone-built folly consisting of three gothic arches. It was built in 1761 to give a focal point to the outlook from Blair Castle but also gives a

beautiful view back to the castle and its landscaped grounds against the Perthshire hills. Return to the main track and carry on down the glen.

The track passes to the left of a house and then down an elegant avenue of trees to reach a minor road. Turn right if you wish to detour to the splendid castle, which also has a restaurant (seasonal opening), or turn left and pass under a stone footbridge to reach the picturesque hamlet of Old Blair. Before heading left along the road, you can detour to the right to explore the ruins of St Bride's Church. Just beyond Old Blair is the crossroads: turn right here to return to the start.

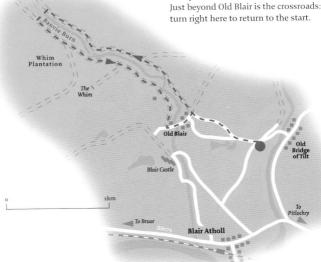

Wilds of Glen Tilt

Distance 6km **Time** 2 hours 30
Terrain good tracks and paths
Maps OS Explorer 386 and 394 **Access** bus
(87) or train from Pitlochry to Blair Atholl,
a short walk from the start

Glen Tilt is a a real gem – all idyllic woods,
clear, rushing water and lofty peaks. This
route, waymarked in green, climbs to a
magnificent viewpoint giving a taste of
the upper glen before looping back along
a pleasant, tree-lined track.

The walk starts from the car park just
beyond the Old Bridge of Tilt. From Blair
Atholl, follow the road north to Old Bridge
of Tilt and left through the village, then
cross the bridge to find the car park on the
left. This approach can also be made on
foot, which adds 3km to the round trip.

Leave the car park by the main entrance
and turn left along the road. Bear right at

the fork to follow the sloping road gently
uphill. On reaching a crossroads, turn right
up a tarmac lane that leads you past
a picturesque pair of estate cottages,
ignoring another lane that branches right.

The road becomes a track as it passes the
castellated farmhouse of Bailanloan below,
with fine views down the glen. Passing
Blairuachdar, the track is lined with
splendid trees as it continues the gradual
climb. Enter the woods and ignore a branch
coming in from the left. Where the route
forks, keep on the lower right-hand track.

Further on, green waymarkers indicate
a sharp right-hand turn onto a less
distinct track heading downhill. Before
going this way, however, carry on along
the main track for about 300m for the
stunning view up Glen Tilt from the
entrance to a rifle range. Back in 1847, this
glen was the scene of an encounter which

◀ Track near Blairuachdar

led to the establishment of a right of way through the glen and the beginning of Scotland's access rights. John Balfour, a professor of botany at the University of Edinburgh, organised field studies for his students in the Highlands each summer. On one such trip down Glen Tilt, he found his way barred by the Duke of Atholl and his ghillies. A violent end to the stand-off was avoided when Balfour and his students climbed over a dyke and ran off, but a lengthy legal case ensued which eventually vindicated Balfour and led to the creation of the Scottish Rights of Way and Recreation Society. This is today known as ScotWays, a campaigning body on access issues which is also responsible for the small green signs pointing out rights of way in the Highlands, many of them ambitious cross-country walks.

Return to the junction to drop down through fine woodland on the track. After a steep section, this crosses a small bridge and makes the gentler descent through birchwoods before reaching the main track up Glen Tilt. Turn right along this. After 1.5km, a waymarker indicates an optional loop off to the left to view the Falls of Fender. The falls are often obscured by foliage and are less impressive than they once were due to the extraction of water

for hydro-electric schemes, but the loop is worthwhile for its woodland scenery alone. Rejoin the track and carry on until another path goes off to the left. Turn left here and cross a stone bridge over the road near the Old Bridge of Tilt to return to the car park.

13

Allean Forest above Loch Tummel

Distance 4km **Time** 1 hour 30
Terrain Clear paths and forest track
**Map OS Explorer 386 Access bus (82) from
Pitlochry to Queen's View Visitor Centre,
a short walk from the start**

**A gentle forest walk above Loch Tummel,
beginning near the famous Queen's View.
The walk has its own viewpoint over the
loch as well as a restored blackhouse and
the remains of a ring fort.**

The Queen's View is a deservedly
popular stopping place. Almost the whole
length of Loch Tummel is framed by
beautiful slopes and the distinctive peak
of Schiehallion; on perfect days, even the
mountains of Glencoe can be picked out in
the far distance. Queen Victoria came here
by carriage in 1866, though the name may
hark back to an earlier visit by Queen
Isabella, wife of Robert the Bruce. Today,

there is a café and visitor centre at the
viewpoint car park.

This walk actually begins from the Allean
Forest car park, just along the road toward
Kinloch Rannoch from the Queen's View,
where there are picnic tables and
composting toilets. Take the marked trail
uphill past the long-drop toilets – which
may be an attraction in itself for some
green-minded visitors – and over a bridge
into the pinewoods. When the path
emerges onto a track, turn left to follow the
red and yellow marker posts. Soon the route
turns right onto another track before
plunging left into the forest on the opposite
side. This path leads over a small bridge and
along a section carpeted with wood
anemone, foxgloves and sorrell in spring
and summer to emerge in a clearing where
you'll find a partially restored blackhouse.
This building would have been typical of

◀ Wooden sculpture by Charlie Easterfield

the village, or *clachan* in Gaelic, with stone walls, a roof of turf or heather, and few windows. There was no chimney, so the walls would have been coated in soot – hence the name – and it would have been home to an entire family. After passing the house, a marker post directs you away from the information board to the left.

Further on, a short detour takes you to a lovely wooden sculpture and a viewpoint over Loch Tummel, with the pointed peak of Schiehallion across the water. Back on the path, cross a wooden bridge and then a track by a short dog-leg to the left. The route now climbs, with open views of the surrounding countryside across a felled area. When this joins a track, head left downhill and ignore a path with a yellow

waymarker on the right. Where the main track curves left, take the right branch with a red marker post. This narrows to a path once again before meeting another track, where you turn right to shortly reach a sign for the ring fort. Here are the remains of a large, circular 8th-century homestead. The earth and stone walls may have once held a roof, supported by wooden poles. Despite the name, ring forts were not primarily defensive structures – and this part of Perthshire has the best remaining examples. After enjoying the peaceful views over Loch Tummel from here, continue downhill by the track to meet the T-junction encountered earlier in the walk. Turn left to return to the car park and the start.

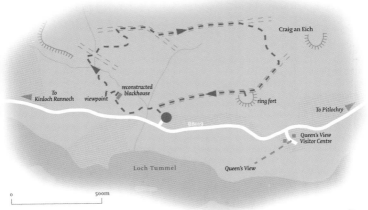

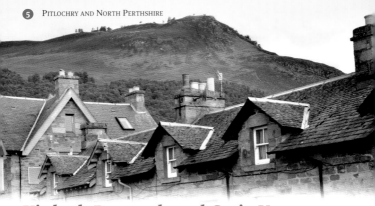

Kinloch Rannoch and Craig Varr

Distance 4km (+4km detour) **Time** 1 hour
(+2 hour detour) **Terrain** **waymarked
forest paths and tracks, fairly level; steep
ascent on optional detour followed by
open ground with some rough and boggy
sections** **Map** OS Explorer 386
Access regular bus (82) from Pitlochry

**This short walk explores the picturesque
village of Kinloch Rannoch, a gateway to
one of the wilder areas of Scotland, with
an optional steep climb to a fantastic
natural viewpoint over the village.**

At the foot of Loch Rannoch, Kinloch
Rannoch is an attractive village seemingly
set in the middle of nowhere. The road to
the west now terminates at Rannoch
Station, but in years gone by the route
continued across the barren landscapes of
Rannoch Moor and beyond – as this was
the famous Road to the Isles. The walk
starts in the attractive square at the centre
of the village where there is some parking.

First, head along the road in the direction
of Pitlochry, passing the petrol station and
garage workshop. Just beyond, turn left up
a lane beside a pretty stone cottage, where
you'll find a waterfall and information
board. Through a gate is a path junction.

The path up the hill marks the start of the
steep and rough ascent of Craig Varr,
with its sensational views over Loch
Rannoch and the surrounding mountains.
This strenuous detour winds up through
the woods; when you reach open ground
turn right at a fork to cross a bridge. Keep to
the obvious route until just beyond a gate,
turning left here to follow a fence and then
stone dyke across boggy ground to the
prow of Craig Varr. Return the same way.

To miss out the detour, turn left where
the Craig Varr path heads uphill and
follow the path marked for Loch Rannoch.
This runs just above the fields, with good
views over the village. Beyond a stone
well, the path shadows the drystone dyke

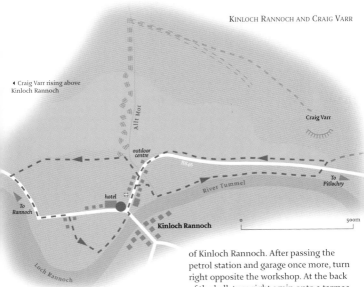

◀ Craig Varr rising above
Kinloch Rannoch

before emerging by houses onto a tarmac road. Turn left to follow this as it curves around the shores of Loch Rannoch.

After a sharp left bend, you come to the edge of the village. Turn right onto a track just after the first cottage and immediately left through a gate. Fork left again by the electricity substation onto a small path. This leads to the sluice gates at the foot of Loch Rannoch. The loch is part of the huge Tummel hydro-power scheme, which was constructed in the 1930s and uses water from all the surrounding glens. The powerful flow of the river is controlled and can rise and fall very quickly.

Follow the path downstream into the woods and pass under the roadbridge, then turn left to head back into the centre

of Kinloch Rannoch. After passing the petrol station and garage once more, turn right opposite the workshop. At the back of the hall, turn right again onto a tarmac path signed for the riverside. Cross a footbridge over a feeder stream and keep to the right of a small housing estate. Leave the tarmac by forking right onto a path through the woods. This soon joins the river on its journey downstream, before ending after a parking area to emerge on the road. Cross this and go through the gate directly opposite, signed for the Hillside Path. As soon as possible, turn very sharp left onto a beautiful path that rises through the edge of the woods, heading back towards the village amongst magnificent trees. Go through a gate and then fork left onto a path that leads down into Kinloch Rannoch, reaching the road next to the outdoor centre. Turn right along the road to return to the start.

Loch Rannoch Forest Walk

Distance **8km** Time **2 hours 30**
Terrain **clear, waymarked forest paths
and tracks** Map OS Explorer 385
Access **postbus (223) from Pitlochry and
Kinloch Rannoch runs along south Loch
Rannoch road; alight at Carie**

**This waymarked circuit combines easy
walking on forest tracks with pleasant
mixed woodland, including remnants of
the ancient Caledonian forest, with good
views over Loch Rannoch.**

The walk sets out from the Forestry
Commission car park at Carie on the south
side of Loch Rannoch. From the far end of
the car park, head for the wooden
footbridge over the falls. Do not cross, but
instead follow the multicoloured marker
posts along the path away from the
bridge. Before reaching the picnic tables
and large shelter, turn right for a gentle

climb. At the next junction, keep right
and then turn left onto a track to pass
pine trees on the left and more open
woodland on the right. At another
junction, follow the yellow marker post
and bear right.

After the Jacobite rebellions of 1690,
1715 and 1745, vast Highland estates were
forfeited by their chiefs and seized by the
crown as punishment for support of the
rebel cause. The Forfeited Estates
Commission was established to oversee
this land and at Carie the commission
operated its own sawmill to harvest the
timber from the Black Wood of Rannoch.

The track rises gently until it is high
above the Allt na Bogair, which can be
glimpsed through the trees on the left as
it tumbles towards Loch Rannoch. Parts
of the forest floor are exposed to the
sunlight here, and blaeberry and bracken

flourish in thick clumps at the side of the path whilst majestic stands of Scots pine tower above. On this section, you'll spy a waterfall far below, a worn patch indicating where people have left the path for a closer look: the banks are very steep here so care is needed. After a while, the path drops down to a footbridge over the water. Rather than cross this, continue on the path that heads up to the right and joins a wide forestry track.

Turn right along this track. (To the left is an isolated route that leads to Glen Lyon via the Lairig Ghallabhaich. It gives a fantastic feeling of remoteness – but hillwalking gear is necessary, as well as transport at the far end.) After a short while, dive into the dense pine trees on the right via a narrow waymarked path, before emerging at another track. Bear right here for a gradual descent, passing a small quarry on the right. To the left, there are excellent views over Loch Rannoch and the empty hills beyond.

Keep an eye out for the next turning onto a path to the right at the corner of a sharp bend in the track. Marked by

two small cairns, the path heads through an area of semi-felled forest. After pausing at a viewpoint, it undulates across the hillside, then drops to rejoin the outward path. Turn left here and left again at the next junction to return to the car park at the start.

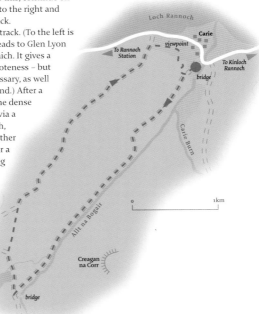

Black Spout and Edradour

Distance 5km **Time** 2 hours
Terrain woodland paths, minor road,
tracks, main road with pavement
Map OS Explorer 386 **Access** Pitlochry is
well served by buses, coaches and trains

This varied walk begins from the centre
of Pitlochry, rising through woodland to
view Black Spout waterfall and visit the
Edradour Distillery, a huddle of pretty
whitewashed buildings, with good views
of the River Tummel and surrounding
hills on the return.

Set off from the tourist information
centre on the main street (Atholl Road) in
the heart of Pitlochry. (There is a car park
here and a smaller one at the start of the
path into Black Spout Wood.) Facing away
from the tourist information centre, turn
left and follow the main road towards

Dunkeld. Where the road passes under the
railway line, divert to the opposite side of
the road and then back again. After passing
the Blair Athol Distillery and a row of
bungalows, turn left uphill (SP Black Spout
Wood) and pass back under the railway.
Keeping to the track on the left, enter the
woods for a gentle ascent, with the Atholl
Palace Hotel golf course over to the left.
At a crossroads, the yellow marker for
Edradour directs you straight on,
eventually bringing you to the Black Spout
viewpoint. The river plunges vertically for
more than 60m here: the falls are
particularly dramatic after heavy rainfall.

The footpath now takes you on a winding
uphill course: keep to the yellow marker
posts and stay right at a fork. It then runs
along the edge of some fields between two
drystone walls, with good views over to

◀ Edradour Distillery

Ben Vrackie on the left. After passing a stone cottage, you emerge at the pretty distillery complex of Edradour. This is the smallest distillery in Scotland, and tours are available during the summer months. With a production of only 12 casks a week, the machinery and stills have remained almost unchanged since the distillery was built in the early 19th century.

Turn left up the road and follow this briefly to find a farm gate just before a set of ornamental stone gateposts on the left. From here, an enclosed, marked path skirts the edge of the field and passes a newly-built house, with fine views over Pitlochry as it starts to descend. Where it joins a grassy track, turn left for Pitlochry. By a house, the route re-enters Black Spout Wood through a kissing gate and

then soon meets a larger track. Turn right here to head downhill, ignoring the slightly earlier path for Milton. In a very short while, at a wide bend, your path branches off to the right (identified by another yellow marker for Pitlochry.) The path crosses a wooden bridge and then bears left along the banks of the Kinnaird Burn. Ignore a path up to the right which leads to the imposing Atholl Palace Hotel.

The next junction is marked by a large triangular stone. Continue to the right here, and keep right again further on. When the path then emerges at the road, turn left to descend to the A924, passing the entrance to the Atholl Palace. At the main road, turn right along the pavement to return to Pitlochry.

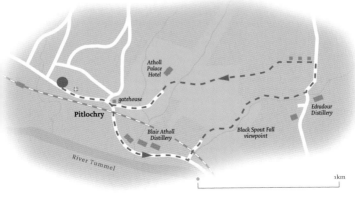

Loch Faskally and the Salmon Ladder

Distance 5km **Time** 2 hours **Terrain** good paths, flights of steps, minor roads
Map OS Explorer 386 **Access** Pitlochry is well served by buses, coaches and trains

A tour of Pitlochry's landmarks, including its well-known suspension bridge, Festival Theatre and salmon ladder, with a loop of Loch Faskally and an option to continue to historic Killiecrankie.

Start from the centre of Pitlochry by the war memorial at the junction of the main street (Atholl Road) and Ferry Road. Walk down Ferry Road, past the memorial gardens and under the railway, curving left to pass a restaurant and guesthouses.

Immediately after the sports field, turn left down a path (SP Festival Theatre and the Fish Ladder) to find the Port-na-Craig Suspension Bridge. Cross this and turn right along the road, passing the Port-na-Craig Inn and the Festival Theatre. Today's famous theatre started life in a large tent

in 1951. The current building opened in 1981 and, as well as a full season of plays, it has a popular café, shop and gardens.

Carry on along the minor road towards the hydro-electric dam, which created Loch Faskally in 1951. An Act of Parliament required the Hydro Board to preserve fish stocks on any waterways affected by the scheme, hence the fish ladder seen on the left side of the dam. It consists of 34 tiered pools with interconnected openings below the waterline to allow fish to swim up into the next pool, and two larger 'rest' pools. One of these has an observation chamber where you can try and spot a migrating salmon through the murky water.

The steps by the observation chamber lead to the top of the dam. Keep left up a few more steps for the circuit of Loch Faskally. At a fork, go right to drop down some steps to the shore, where a clear path skirts the water's edge with one deviation down and then up a long flight

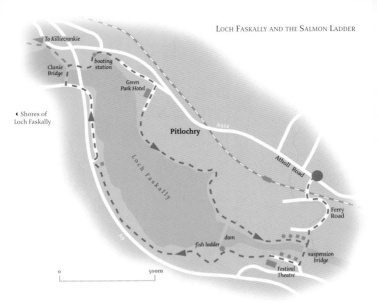

◀ Shores of
Loch Faskally

of steps to cross a bridge. The path soon leaves the water and approaches the thunderingly busy A9. Stay in the woods to eventually pass a house at Balmore and meet a minor road, which you accompany gently downhill to the right. After passing under the A9 bridge, take an immediate right over a footbridge with good views to the left where the loch widens again.

If you wish to detour along the rest of the loch and the River Garry to Killiecrankie and the famous Soldier's Leap (5km), turn left here and follow the green waymarkers, keeping the water on your left. The path eventually leads to the visitor centre, where you can catch a bus for the 10-minute ride back to Pitlochry: check the timetable first.

For the main route, turn right on the far side of the bridge, passing back under the A9. After a boating station and waterside café, go straight on to join a road which climbs past the Green Park Hotel. Immediately after the hotel, turn right down a narrow path (SP Pitlochry Dam), passing through lovely woodland. Keep to the main path nearest the water, ignoring any tracks coming in from the left.

At a gap in a fence, some steps take you down towards the dam. Cross the minor road and climb the steps on the far side to continue through the woodland before emerging at an open grassy area. The route leads between the river and houses, turning left when you arrive back at the suspension bridge. Retrace your steps to the centre of Pitlochry.

Craigower over Pitlochry

Distance 5km Time 2 hours
Terrain clear paths, steep at times
Map OS Explorer 386 Access bus (24)
from Pitlochry to Moulin, 1.5km away;
Pitlochry is well served by buses, coaches
and trains

**This short walk takes as its objective
a wooded summit 400m above Pitlochry,
a superb spot with wide-ranging views to
Loch Tummel, Rannoch and, on a clear
day, even the peaks of Glencoe. It is also a
locally important habitat for butterflies.**

The route starts from the small car park
at Craigower, and is waymarked. Access by
car is via the A924 northbound from
Pitlochry, turning left immediately after
the Moulin Inn to follow the road round
to the car park at Balnacraig. To walk from
Pitlochry itself, which adds 3km to the
round trip, climb Larchwood Road, passing

a former curling pond known as The Cuilc
and then the golf clubhouse. At the top of
the road, turn left to reach the car park.

Take the track that leads around
Balnacraig Steading to the golf course.
Cross this, bearing right at the fork and
keeping a watchful eye out for golfballs as
you cross the fairway to reach the fourth
tee. There are great views from here back
over the fine stone houses of Pitlochry
and the countryside around it. A sign
guides you left along a fenced path.

The path overlooks the golf course
initially before diving into the woods
for a gentle climb. Cross a track diagonally
to find the marked path on the other side
and steel yourself for the much steeper
climb through dense forestry, before
emerging onto more open heathland
scattered with Scots pine. This is the
summit of Craigower, owned by the

◂ Looking back over the golf course towards Pitlochry

National Trust for Scotland. It is an important habitat for butterflies, and you may be lucky enough to spot the brilliantly-named Green Hairstreak in the spring or the Scotch Argus in late summer. Some wooden steps take you up to the flat top of Craigower, where a seat to the left enjoys a fabulous outlook to Pitlochry while to the right is Loch Tummel and the iconic peak of Schiehallion.

It was the regular shape and isolated position of Schiehallion that gave it its place in history as the spot where contour lines were invented. In 1774, Nevil Maskelyne, the Astronomer Royal, became the first to measure the mass of the earth, which he did by observing the deflection of a pendulum by the mass of Schiehallion. As part of the experiment, the volume of Schiehallion had to be calculated, for which purpose contours were invented by the geologist Charles Hutton, and have been used ever since to represent landscapes on 2D maps.

The waymarked central path continues with a climb up a couple of steps to join a forest track. Turn right along this, passing a communications mast as you meander steadily downhill. At a junction, turn left to rejoin the outward path through the woods and across the golf course to the start of the walk.

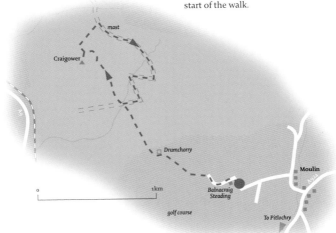

mast

Craigower

Drumchorry

Moulin

Balnacraig
Steading

To Pitlochry

0   1km

golf course

Ben Vrackie

Distance 8.5km **Time** 4 hours
Terrain good hill path with a steep ascent
to the summit; hillwalking gear is needed
Map OS Explorer 386 **Access** bus (24) from
Pitlochry to Moulin, 1.5km away, then
500m walk along Baledmund Road

Ben Vrackie is the small mountain that is
indelibly associated with Pitlochry: on
a clear day, the views are magnificent.
This route takes in woods, moorland and
a pretty lochan with a final, steep climb
and an optional 2km loop. The upper
sections are exposed, so full hillwalking
clothing, map and compass are essential.

Ben Vrackie's name, meaning 'Speckled
Mountain' in Gaelic, is attributed to the
vibrant mix of heather and grey stone on
its flanks. At 841m high, it is classed as one
of the 219 Scottish Corbetts, which are
growing in popularity as an objective for
walkers who have completed or want an
alternative to the higher Munros. Ben
Vrackie is easier than most and appeals to
a much wider range of walkers.

There is a small car park at the start of
the walk which is just northwest of
Moulin, 1.5 km from Pitlochry. To reach
this, turn left off the A924 just behind the
Moulin Hotel and follow the road uphill,
continuing straight ahead when it goes
left, to reach a car park after 300m on the
right. From the car park, a well-signed path
climbs through the mixed woodland. As
you continue to rise, you cross a track,
skirt around the woodland and turn left
onto a small track. Go over another
forestry track, following the path across a
bridge over the Moulin Burn and through
the trees, before finally emerging onto the
open moor via a gate.

Ben Vrackie

To Killiecrankie

Loch a'Choire

Bealach na Searmoin

Meall na h-Aodainn Moire

reservoir

Meall Uaine

Creag Bhreac

Baledmund

Balnakeilly

Moulin

A924

To Pitlochry

0   1km

seat, keeping to the path as it crosses the small dam and then the outlet burn via stepping stones.

Now the hard part begins. The climb to the summit is steep but the path is good, having been recently pitched with stone to counteract the erosion caused by so many boots on this popular hill. At the top is a viewpoint indicator and, on a clear day, you can see Ben Lawers and Schiehallion, Beinn a'Ghlo and many other Cairngorms peaks from here. On a day of exceptional visibility, it is claimed that a keen eye will pick out Arthur's Seat in Edinburgh.

The easiest and quickest route of return is to retrace your steps on the main path. However, it is possible to detour around Loch a'Choire on a quieter moorland route for part of the way. To do this, go back down the steep section of path until just before the outlet for Loch a'Choire. Here, take the clear path branching off to the right and skirt around the edge of the loch. This path can be wet underfoot until it begins to climb gently through heather beyond the water. Keep on the main path, ignoring a path to the left.

As the path narrows, you get some good views towards Blair Atholl. Descend to an obvious junction, where there is a sign for Killiecrankie to the right. Turn left here for the gradual ascent to gain the lowest point between the two hills, the Bealach na Searmoin. Here, you begin to descend to rejoin the outward route. Turn right to return downhill to the start of the walk.

As you cross this heather moorland, Ben Vrackie comes into view for the first time. There is also a good outlook back to Pitlochry and across the River Tummel. Stay on the main path, ignoring a fork to the left. The branch-off is part of the Bealach Walk and can be used as the return route if you choose to make the optional extension around Loch a'Choire. Go through another gate to follow a path up a gentle incline. After rounding a corner, it starts to dip down towards the loch where, on the far side, the steep path can be seen snaking up the side of Ben Vrackie. Pass a beautifully carved wooden

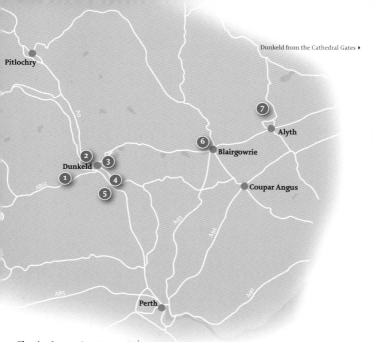

Dunkeld from the Cathedral Gates ▶

Pitlochry

⑦

Alyth

②
Dunkeld ③ ⑥ Blairgowrie
①
④
⑤

Coupar Angus

Perth

The tiny but ancient town of Dunkeld
is at the heart of Perthshire and was once
the ecclesiastical capital of Scotland. The
relics of St Columba himself were kept
here when Iona fell to Viking raiders.

Today, the pretty whitewashed cottages,
attractive wynds and independent shops
gather round the Cross and stretch down
to the grand Telford bridge over the River
Tay, whilst the ruins of the cathedral are
a reminder of a more illustrious past.

Dunkeld is a great location from which
to explore the region. Nearby is the famed
Hermitage and Ossian's Hall, part of which
was in the 18th century one of the most

important designed landscapes in
Scotland, visited by J M W Turner, William
Wordsworth and Sir Walter Scott. It is also
possible to walk from Dunkeld to Loch of
the Lowes, where a telescope allows you to
view the eyrie of the majestic osprey, once
driven to extinction from Britain.

Just over the hills to the east is fertile
Strathmore and the wilder Glen Shee,
where Perthshire meets the Cairngorms.
Blairgowrie is the main centre here, with
its long history in the linen trade, whilst
neighbouring Alyth sits on the eastern
fringes of the county.

Dunkeld and Blairgowrie

Braan Walk and the Hermitage

Distance 6.5km **Time** 2 hours
Terrain good paths and tracks
Map OS Explorer 379 **Access** bus or
train to Birnam, 1km from the start

A fine circular walk to visit the waterfalls
of the Hermitage and the curious follies
of Ossian's Hall and Cave. To start this
route from the centre of Dunkeld, follow
the signs for Inver.

Begin from the Inver car park, southeast
of the small village of Inver off the A9,
opposite Dunkeld (not the car park signed
for the Hermitage). You'll find walk details
on the information board here. Take the
lower path signed Braan Walk to enter the
woods. Stick to the higher, waymarked
path where it forks, keeping an eye out for
red squirrels as you make your way
upstream along the River Braan, passing a
carved memorial bench along the way.

Near the riverbank, just before you come
to a stone bridge, is a contender for the

title of Britain's tallest tree. At a lofty
61.3m, this Douglas Fir currently stands in
third place but as the trees are still
growing, the race is not over yet.

Cross the bridge over the dramatic Black
Linn waterfall, which can also be viewed
by passing through a tunnel under the
bridge. On the far side is Ossian's Hall, the
centrepiece of The Hermitage, a wild
garden built by the son-in-law of the
second Duke of Atholl in 1758. Ossian's
Hall is usually open and, in addition to the
viewing platform, contains mirrored
images from *The Poems of Ossian*. The hall
was built as a viewing house for the falls
and redecorated as a shrine to Ossian in
1783. The 'works' of the mythical Ossian
were an epic romantic cycle of poems,
published by James MacPherson in 1765,
supposedly having been discovered and
translated from ancient Celtic texts. The
works became hugely influential, popular
amongst many of Europe's elite from Sir

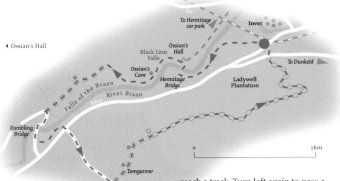

◄ Ossian's Hall

Walter Scott to Napoleon, but today's scholars agree with Samuel Johnson's opinion that the poems were largely the work of MacPherson himself.

The romantic theme was extended to the inner room of the hall, which was originally lined with mirrors, giving visitors the impression of water cascading from all directions. William Wordsworth visited and wrote a poem describing the 'world of wonder' of the room. In 1869, part of the hall was blown up by vandals and the building fell into decay. Recently the National Trust for Scotland, which now owns the Hermitage, has restored it.

From the hall, turn left and proceed along the wide path for grand views of the tumbling river. Soon you reach Ossian's Cave, another folly built as part of the Hermitage. Continue straight ahead, sticking to the path nearest the river. At a crossroads, turn left and follow the green marker posts through the woods to reach a track. Turn left again to pass a pretty cottage, and go over a bridge and through a gate. The track crosses open grazing land before coming to a road, which you follow to the left to find the tumultuous cascade beneath the Rumbling Bridge. This waterfall is a good place to spot leaping salmon in late autumn, especially after heavy rain. After crossing the bridge, take the first path on the left, which gives good views back along the river. It emerges from the woods at a road, which you go straight across to carry on along a track.

As the track rises, turn left at a fork and curve to the right, past the house at Tomgarrow. Pass a caravan and go through a gate into a woodland of birch and pine. Just before another house, fork right and cross a small bridge and gate to enter Ladywell Plantation. When the path reaches a forestry track, turn left, noting the green markers. Keep on the main track, ignoring a branch on the right, to meet another track. A left turn here takes you to the road. Cross this to return to the start.

King's Seat and the Dunkeld larches

Distance 4.5km **Time** 2 hours
Terrain woodland paths, can be muddy
Map OS Explorer 379 **Access** Dunkeld is
well served by buses and coaches; train
station at nearby Birnam

**This walk explores historic Dunkeld and
the birthplace of modern forestry, taking
in the King's Seat viewpoint and the only
surviving specimen of the first larch trees
to be planted in Britain.**

The name Dunkeld comes from the
Gaelic *Dùn Chailleann*, meaning the 'Fort of
the Caledonians', and it refers to a fort
that once stood at King's Seat. Originally
founded by the king of the Picts, the
settlement has a rich history. It was
almost totally destroyed during the Battle
of Dunkeld in 1869, when the Jacobites
were beaten after their victory at the Battle
of Killiecrankie. Musket ball holes from
the battle can still be seen in the cathedral
walls. The main street (Atholl Street) was

built in Georgian times to complement
Thomas Telford's bridge over the Tay and
is full of interesting shops and cafés.

Begin the walk from the far corner of the
car park at the north end of Atholl Street.
A waymarked path starts here, passing to
the right of Stanley Hill. Head straight
across the surfaced path and then turn left
onto the minor road beyond: this is the
driveway to the Dunkeld House Hotel,
a one-time home of the Dukes of Atholl.

After some distance, a blue waymarker
guides you onto a path bound for the
woods on the right. The path runs above
the road until it meets a track which is
followed to the right. This can be muddy
as it is sometimes used for Landrover
expeditions. At a fork, turn right and then
left at the next junction, keeping close to
the edge of the wood. Bear right at the
next two junctions. Just before a minor
road, go left down a broad track and then
right at the next fork to follow a slender

◀ Larches by the River Tay

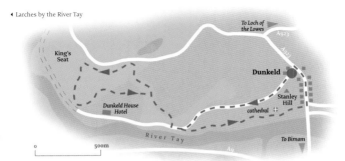

track which rises into the trees. In a while, a waymarked path leads you off to the right to find a wooden bench beneath the cliff: this is the King's Seat. The viewpoint is a little further on, a site chosen for its sweeping views of the strath below, though now partly obscured by trees.

Beyond the viewpoint is a T-junction: turn left to follow a track as it curves left and passes above some new houses before crossing the access drive. Keep to the right at the next section where, after a slight rise, you join another route coming in from the right. At the next junction, bear right to enter the Amphitheatre, a dell encircled by tall fir trees. The route skirts around the edge of this until, at a large tree, you turn right onto the outward route. Return along this until you reach some wooden steps and a path down to the road. Cross straight over this and turn left onto the track running parallel to but well above the mighty River Tay.

Here, you can admire Dunkeld's famous larches: as you approach the cathedral, you will find the Parent Larch or Mother

Tree, the only survivor of five seedlings planted here in 1738, the first larches in Britain. They were used as the source of seeds for the extensive forestry planting that took place initially in Perthshire and eventually much of Scotland. The third and fourth Dukes of Atholl planted 14 million larches from the seeds of this tree and its siblings.

Walk left along the cathedral's perimeter fence: you can enter the grounds of the partially ruined medieval structure at the far end. The cathedral choir is still in use as the parish church and contains the tomb of Alexander Stewart, the notorious Wolf of Badenoch who burnt Elgin Cathedral in 1390 before a stint behind bars reformed him: his black marble monument can be seen here. The Chapter House holds a museum. If you can tear yourself away from the cathedral and its beautiful riverside setting, head through the wrought iron gates into Dunkeld. Go down the road past the carved memorial fountain of the Cross to reach the main street, turning left to return to the start.

Loch of the Lowes from the Fungarth

Distance 8km **Time** 2 hours 30
Terrain paths, track and minor road
Map OS Explorer 379 **Access** Dunkeld is
well served by buses and coaches; train
station at nearby Birnam

This waymarked circuit explores the
rolling countryside north of Dunkeld and
offers the chance to watch the famous
ospreys at the Loch of the Lowes. A hide
(admission fee) managed by the Scottish
Wildlife Trust is equipped with spotting
scopes overlooking the eyrie. The route
also explores Dunkeld, which can be used
as an alternative start point.

The walk starts at the Cally car park, 1km
north of historic Dunkeld on a track off

the A923 to Blairgowrie. From the entrance
to the car park, head straight across onto
the track opposite (SP Fungarth Walk).
After a short while, take the grassy track
which dives into the trees on the right. At
a fork, waymarkers guide you left through
fine beechwoods on a path which runs
parallel to before joining the busy A923.

Cross the road, turning briefly right and
then left up the lane towards the golf club.
At the far end of the club car park, take the
track signposted for the Fungarth Walk.
Cross a grassy field to a kissing gate and
continue along the track through a
wooden gate. The pleasantly wooded
route leads past a cottage before swinging
left and rising to join another lovely old
track running across the hillside.

From here, it is worth detouring to the Loch of the Lowes. Follow the lane left downhill to reach a minor road. Cross this and join the path on the far side, which runs through the trees just to the right of the road with glimpses out over the water. After a short distance, you'll come to the parking area for the Scottish Wildlife Trust reserve. The main attraction here is the nesting ospreys which can be seen between April and August. However, there is also a huge variety of birds both on the loch and around the feeders by the visitor centre. The entry fee includes the use of powerful telescopes and live CCTV footage beamed from the osprey eyrie itself. Ospreys are a real success story for this part of Perthshire. Having been persecuted and hunted to extinction in Britain, they returned to the area to nest in 1969. Round-the-clock supervision of the nest site and perseverance on the part of the SWT, RSPB and other conservation bodies to improve water quality, provide better habitats and prevent illegal killing and egg thieving has paid off. Since 1991, the current female has successfully fledged 43 chicks here, and it is a breathtaking spectacle to see these magnificent birds for real. The siskins, woodpeckers and red squirrels around the feeding area are also entertaining, and you can watch them from the comfort of the visitor centre.

Return uphill to the point where you left the track earlier, this time carrying straight on for Dunkeld. When you meet a tarmac road, steer right and right again at some houses. The approach to Dunkeld is downhill, with good views over the town's fine 18th-century buildings and cottages to the cathedral. Turn right along the main street. Unless you wish to explore Dunkeld's super blend of shops, cafés and pubs, simply follow the road out through the town, passing the ornate gateway to the Dunkeld House Hotel on the far side. At the T-junction with the main road, turn right towards Blairgowrie: take care as there is no pavement on this short section. The second turning on the left, beside an attractive cottage, takes you back to the Cally car park.

◀ The Loch of the Lowes and the osprey eyrie

A spell on the Tay to Birnam

Distance 6km **Time** 1 hour 30
Terrain riverside paths and roads
Map OS Explorer 379 **Access** Dunkeld is
well served by buses and coaches; train
station at nearby Birnam

**An easy waymarked circuit taking in the
ancient Birnam Oak and a lovely stretch
of the River Tay before returning through
Birnam, where you can visit the Institute
with its art gallery, café and enchanting
Beatrix Potter exhibition and garden.**

The walk begins at the Taybank Hotel,
the renowned folk music hub, in Dunkeld.
Cross the fine Dunkeld Bridge over the
Tay before turning down a flight of stone
steps on the left, next to the tiny former
tollhouse, and heading downstream
along the riverbank.

The Tay is Scotland's longest and
mightiest river, beginning its journey as
the River Cononish on the slopes of Ben
Lui, just 32km from Oban – nearer to the
west than east coast. It becomes the Tay

as it flows from Loch Tay and, by the time
it reaches Dunkeld, its wide waters are
renowned amongst anglers for salmon-
fishing. During the salmon season, from
mid-January to the end of November,
you're likely to spot fishing boats as well
as wader-clad fly fishermen waist-deep in
water. Sometimes salmon can be seen
leaping out of the water as they head
upstream to spawn. It is an even more
amazing sight when you consider that
those same fish, having spent their early
life on the river, will have since completed
an epic journey to the saltwater feeding
grounds of the North Sea and the Atlantic.
Some may have reached the west coast of
Greenland before returning, a distance of
almost 10,000km as the crow flies.

After passing a turning area and crossing
a small bridge, you arrive at the Birnam
Oak, the third in a series of magnificent
trees along this stretch. Supported by
wooden stilts, it is said to be the last
remaining tree from Birnam Wood, made

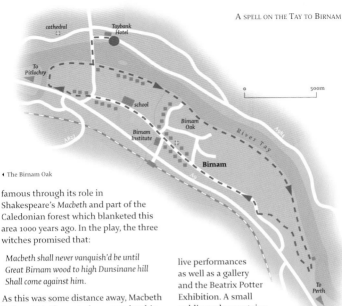

◀ The Birnam Oak

famous through its role in Shakespeare's *Macbeth* and part of the Caledonian forest which blanketed this area 1000 years ago. In the play, the three witches promised that:

*Macbeth shall never vanquish'd be until
Great Birnam wood to high Dunsinane hill
Shall come against him.*

As this was some distance away, Macbeth believed his throne to be secure, but his enemies attacked after approaching Dunsinane camouflaged in branches from the wood, and Macbeth was overthrown.

Keep following the main path beyond the oak, ignoring the turning into Birnam. Further on, some spectacularly large beech trees line the riverside. At a fishing jetty and hut, make a right turn onto a track which leads you slightly away from the water to meet a road. Cross this to go through the kissing gate opposite and another one beyond, where you now turn right onto the road and accompany it all the way through Birnam. In the village centre, on the left, you'll see the Birnam Institute – home to an excellent café and

live performances as well as a gallery and the Beatrix Potter Exhibition. A small public garden contains bronze sculptures of Potter's characters: the artist and writer spent much time in this area as a young woman and a letter she wrote here led to the creation of *The Tale of Peter Rabbit*.

At the junction after the school, go straight across the main road and follow the minor road opposite, passing the offices of the World Wildlife Fund. The road soon becomes a surfaced path which leads you to the River Braan. Turn right to shadow the Braan to the point where it shortly joins the River Tay, with a splendid views across the water to the cathedral. At Dunkeld Bridge, return up the steps by the tollhouse and cross the bridge to the start.

Birnam Hill and Stair Bridge

Distance 6km **Time** 2 hours 30
Terrain rough paths, some boggy ground,
very steep descent **Map** OS Explorer 379
Access footpath from train station in
Birnam or bus (23) to Birnam Quarry

**This more strenuous circuit rewards with
an enchanting outlook over Dunkeld and
the surrounding countryside. The ascent
to the viewpoint is long and reasonably
gentle, but the descent is very steep.**

The walk starts at the Birnam Quarry
layby just off the A9 on the B867, 1km
south of Birnam. It is possible to reach
this walk on foot from the train station at
Birnam by passing under the railway and
turning left via the red marker signs,
joining the route at the bottom of the
descent from Birnam Hill.

From the parking area, walk under the
railway and follow the track for a very
short distance, looking out for a signed

turning on the left. Keep to the path as it
climbs steadily through mixed woodland.
Further on, there are views over the
railway line as the path accompanies a
fence and then a wall uphill, before
levelling off as it starts to curve around
the slopes to the right. At a junction, the
route continues to the right but you can
make a short detour to Stair Bridge by
going straight on. This ancient stone
bridge gives magical views down the glen
towards Rohallion Lodge, a fairytale
turreted castle set by a loch and forest.
Return to the main route and continue
around the flank of Birnam Hill.

The path soon leaves the trees and
crosses open heather moorland. This is a
good area for spotting birds of prey such
as buzzard, merlin and sometimes the rare
hen harrier. The birds can often be heard
calling to each other as they circle above
the crags. The path contours around the

◄ On Birnam Hill

knoll ahead before climbing, gently at first and then up steps, to reach the top of the King's Seat. Here, there is a large cairn and fantastic views over the rich, green woodland and pasture that make up this classic Perthshire landscape.

From the top, a distinct path drops downhill. There are a couple of rocky sections near the top which require care, and then a boggy area, before good views over Dunkeld and Birnam are revealed from a rocky crag. The path now begins a steep descent through woods. Further down, you may be grateful to find a seat as the path is unrelentingly steep and can be slippery after rain. Keep an eye out for mountain bikers who may be hanging on for dear life as they tear down this section. At the bottom, turn right onto a wide path which soon turns into a track and then a road which passes between houses. Keep right at any junctions.

Beyond the houses, you'll see a sign marking the track ahead as private. This route turns left just before the sign to access a marked path which meanders through the woods, crossing a small wooden bridge at one point. This part of the walk can be noisy at times, as it runs

close to the busy A9. Keep following the path until it emerges onto a track. The route goes straight across this to continue on a pathway: if, however, it appears to be too boggy, an alternative is to simply walk down the track, as the path rejoins it later.

Assuming you have taken the path, turn right when you re-emerge on the track for a gentle descent which passes back under the railway to the start of the walk.

Cargill's Leap and the Knockie

Distance 6km **Time** 2 hours
Terrain waymarked paths, tracks and
minor roads **Map** OS Explorer 381
Access Blairgowrie is well served by buses
from Perth and Dundee

**This varied circuit follows the River Ericht
upstream, with waterfalls, woodland and
old mills along the way. The return is over
the Knockie, a viewpoint which looks out
over Blairgowrie to the Sidlaw Hills.**

Blairgowrie owes much of its past
prosperity to the power of the River Ericht,
explored on this walk. The town was built
around the textile industry which
harnessed the fast-flowing water to run
mills spinning flax, some weaving it into
linen and others processing jute.

This walk starts at the riverside car park
on the north side of the centre, where
you'll find an information board and
picnic tables. To access on foot, go down

the steps next to the bridge, passing the
steel fish sculpture. From the car park,
follow the path signed for Cargill's Leap
upstream. After a fairly short distance, the
path goes left up a flight of wooden steps
to reach an upper track. Turn right along
this, now high above the river.

On the right, a flight of wooden steps
down to a viewing platform makes
a good detour. Continue along the track
before branching off on the right to a
second viewing platform overlooking a
series of cataracts in the river below. This
is Cargill's Leap, where Donald Cargill, a
local minster and covenanter, escaped
pursuing troops by leaping the falls. He
was eventually captured and, after uttering
his final words 'Death to the believer is
just like putting off a worn suit of clothes,
and putting on a new suit', he was
executed in July 1681.

Return from Cargill's Leap to the main

◀ Mill on the River Ericht

path. When it forks, it is worth detouring along the right-hand branch to a long, narrow wooden footbridge spanning the river. Upstream is a weir which once helped channel water to drive the wheels, whilst on both sides of the river are some of the textile mills that made Blairgowrie prosperous. In 1860 there were 11 water-powered mills, employing 1600 people in the town. Today, the grand old flax mill on the east side of the river, Keathbank Mill, has been converted into apartments, whilst the one on the west side is derelict. Do not cross the river, but instead return to the track running upstream. Pass some old millworkers' cottages and then Brooklinn Mill, now a private home.

At the minor road, turn left for a gentle climb past Lornty Farm, turning right onto a track at the next junction to continue to rise through rich mixed farmland. This part of Perthshire, and neighbouring Angus, has long been associated with soft-fruit farming, now grown in plastic polytunnels which scatter the landscape.

Eventually, a wooden signpost indicates a path to the left, an often muddy route which leads through a gap in a fence to a

bench and view indicator. This is the Knockie, a fine viewpoint for Blairgowrie, Strathmore and the Sidlaw Hills. A grassy lane winds down the hill, passing first some newer houses and then an old farmhouse, before swinging left to reach the end of Burnhead Road. Turn right onto Newton Street here, going straight through several crossroads and all the way down to the High Street. Turn left along this, keeping with it as it bends right, to reach the top of the Wellmeadow. You'll find the riverside car park down a lane on the left.

Cateran Trail to the Hill of Alyth

Distance 6.5km **Time** 2 hours 30
Terrain minor road, track and moorland
path, boggy and indistinct in places; a
steep climb **Map** OS Explorer 381
Access bus (57) from Blairgowrie, Perth
and Dundee

**Two hills for just one climb is the bargain
claim of this circuit. Starting in Alyth, the
route climbs steeply, but is rewarded by
fantastic views of the Sidlaw Hills to the
south and the Cairngorms to the north.**

Alyth is a fine little town with a history
stretching back to the 11th century. The
walk begins from the parking area in the
centre, crossing the burn and turning left
to follow the east bank past the Alyth
Hotel and the Alyth Museum. At the far
end is a packhorse bridge, thought to date
from 1500. Continue along Toutie Street
and up the steep rise before turning right
into Hill Street at the top. Bear left into
Loyal Road, following the green signs for
the 102km Cateran Trail, which mostly

follows old drovers' routes through the
countryside around Blairgowrie. It is
named after the gangs of cattle thieves
known as Caterans who flourished in this
part of the Highlands from the middle
ages until well into the 17th century.

After passing the entrance to the Lands
of Loyal Hotel on the right, go through a
metal gate and follow the track for a short,
steep climb with ever-improving views
back over Strathmore and the Sidlaw Hills.

The gradient eases a little before
steepening for a final push to the crest of
the hill. At the three gates, turn right to
enter the one into the wood and make the
short climb to the top of the Hill of Loyal.
Don't follow the track which hugs the wall
but bear slightly to the right, aiming for
the highest ground through trees and
then gorse bushes. There are a number of
faint cattle paths and rabbit runs, so it is
best to keep heading for the top of the hill.
Once the gorse gives way to heather, the
going is easier. At the summit, it is worth

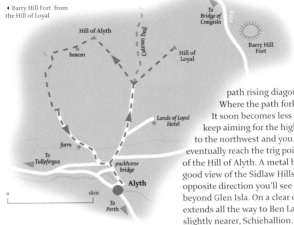

◀ Barry Hill Fort from the Hill of Loyal

To Bridge of Craigisla

Barry Hill Fort

Hill of Alyth

beacon

Cateran Trail

Hill of Loyal

Lands of Loyal Hotel

farm

To Tullyfergus

packhorse bridge

Alyth

0   1km

To Perth

path rising diagonally uphill. Where the path forks, keep right. It soon becomes less distinct, but keep aiming for the highest ground to the northwest and you should eventually reach the trig point at the top of the Hill of Alyth. A metal bench gives a good view of the Sidlaw Hills, while in the opposite direction you'll see the hills beyond Glen Isla. On a clear day, the view extends all the way to Ben Lawers and, slightly nearer, Schiehallion.

dropping slightly to the east, where there are some pine trees and a fence, for an aerial view of the rings of the fort on neighbouring Barry Hill. Legend suggests that this fort may have been the castle where the Pictish King Mordred took Queen Guinevere prisoner following the defeat of her husband King Arthur. Scottish tradition states that Guinevere did not find her captor as repugnant as might be thought and that King Arthur, on learning of his wife's infidelity, was so enraged that he ordered that she be torn to pieces by wild horses: she is supposedly buried nearby. Archaeologists have since dismissed Barry Hill's place in history by deciding the fort is not ancient enough to have played this part in the tale.

Return to the gate and this time go right through a pedestrian gate. Ignore the sign for the Cateran Trail and take the grassy

After a short distance, bear left, heading for a large wooden beacon which will guide you through a maze of paths to pick up a larger westbound track nearby. Around here are good views over Alyth.

The track drops down through the gorse over boggy ground to the corner of a fence. A path keeps right of the fence to climb towards a stand of pine trees, passing a marker post. Beyond the trees, go straight on through a waymarked wooden gate. The boggy path now descends through fields. Turn left at the bottom onto a track, and accompany this as it swings right and descends towards Alyth. Pass to the left of some farm buildings and bear left along a road, turning left at the T-junction to reach the top of the first hill you climbed on the way out of Alyth. Retrace your steps through the town to the start.

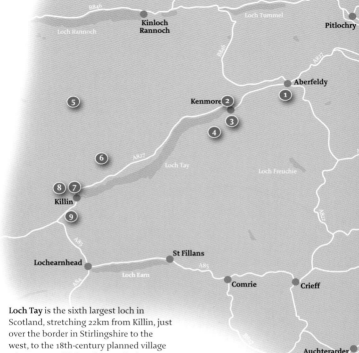

Loch Tay is the sixth largest loch in Scotland, stretching 22km from Killin, just over the border in Stirlingshire to the west, to the 18th-century planned village of Kenmore with its whitewashed cottages and elegant bridge to the east. The loch is scattered with tiny man-made islands, or crannogs, defensive dwellings dating back to the Iron Age.

To the north of Loch Tay is the mighty Ben Lawers mountain range, concealing behind it Glen Lyon, which was described by Sir Walter Scott as the 'longest, loneliest and loveliest glen in Scotland'. Today, it is still a peaceful retreat well worth venturing off the beaten track for.

The largest settlement in this area is further east at Aberfeldy, a handsome, stone-built town tightly clustered around its central square. Its showplace is the Birks, an enchanting wooded ravine whose waterfalls are celebrated in song by Robert Burns. This whole area also forms part of the historic district of Breadalbane, meaning High Country: you'll see frequent references to this locally.

Breadalbane Park, Killin ▶

Killin, Kenmore and Aberfeldy

The Birks of Aberfeldy

Distance 3.5km **Time** 1 hour 30
Terrain narrow paths, steps and steep
sections **Map** OS Explorer 379 **Access**
Aberfeldy is well served by buses

**This very popular short walk heads up the
Moness gorge to visit the series of
waterfalls immortalised in the Burns
ballad 'The Birks of Aberfeldy'. The birch,
oak, ash and elms which cling to the
gorge are spectacular in the autumn.**

The walk begins from the Birks car
park,which is accessed by a signed path
from the main square in Aberfeldy if
setting out on foot. From the upper car
park, take the obvious trail, bearing left to
cross the large bridge over the foaming
Moness Burn. This lower part of the Birks
is predominantly a beechwood; it becomes
more varied as the soil quality changes
further up.

Whilst there were great forests in this
area when man first arrived about 5000

years ago, the woods that are here today
were planted much later. The original
Caledonian forest was cleared for timber
and to make space for growing crops. In
fact, deforestation in Scotland was so
complete that when Dr Johnson toured
the country in 1773 he commented that 'a
tree in Scotland was as rare as a horse in
Venice'. Towards the end of the 18th
century, landowners began to replant as
the economic value of timber increased
and trees became fashionable as part of a
'scenic' landscape. Records show that the
gorge, then called the Den of Moness, was
planted in the late 1780s. Some of the trees
that cling to the the steep sides are likely
to be relics of the original forest, however,
as their inaccessibility means they were
unlikely to have been cut down or grazed.

The walk follows the clear path beside
the burn, passing several small waterfalls.
(The walking trail, the Rob Roy Way, also
shares this trail as the approach to

◀ Moness Burn

Aberfeldy.) As it narrows into the gorge, the path has a handrail. Cross a bridge over a feeder burn with attractive falls on the left. Just beyond is a natural shelf in the rocks known as Burns' Seat. It was here that Robert Burns is said to have taken a rest when he visited in 1787. The visit inspired his ballad 'The Birks of Aberfeldy' and, following the rise in popularity of the den (meaning 'wooded glen' in Scots), the Moness Estate built a path and opened it up to the public. As you gain height, the large beech trees are left behind to be replaced by ash, wych elm, hazel and willow in the wetter spots. These damp conditions are also perfect for mosses: there are at least 10 different species just around Burns' Seat alone.

The climb continues up several flights of stone steps and switchbacks, with views over a series of cascades, before following the wooden walkway up the gorge. At the end of this, the path forks. Detour straight ahead to reach a viewpoint for the Middle Falls, where the Moness Burn flows through a ravine. Afterwards, return to the path, where a brief clearing soon gives a good view of the dramatic Upper Moness Falls. This landscape, with its steep sided U-shaped valleys, was carved by retreating glaciers during the last ice age 10,000 years ago. The glaciers left steep drops from hanging valleys like the one the waterfall tumbles over today. Next, the path crosses the footbridge over

the Upper Falls. If you have a head for heights, this is a spot to appreciate the power of the water as tree trunks, swept down in earlier spates, lie smashed on the gorge floor far below.

The path now bears right to return down the other side of the gorge. The woodland here is mostly birches, or 'birks' in Scots. Together with rowan and willow, these trees can tolerate poor soils and windy conditions. The descent gives plenty of good tree-framed views and is easy to follow back to the car park.

Black Rock from Kenmore

Distance **7km** Time **2 hours**
Terrain **waymarked tracks, paths**
Map **OS Explorer 379** Access **bus (893)
from Aberfeldy and Killin**

**Combine two waymarked walks on
Drummond Hill to visit the stunning
Black Rock viewpoint over Loch Tay and
glimpse huge Taymouth Castle. This hill
is also home to the rare capercaillie.**

After the First World War, Drummond
Hill was one of the first sites to be bought
by the new Forestry Commission which
was set up to replant the forestry felled for
timber as part of the war effort. Prior to
this, the hill had been used for forestry
experiments and was chosen as the
reintroduction site for the capercaillie in
1837, the bird having previously been
hunted to extinction in Britain. Thanks to
the extensive covering of Scots pine, the
capercaillie has continued to thrive on
Drummond Hill, although the bird is still
endangered and, given its shy nature,

rarely seen. You stand a better chance of
hearing one: the distinctive clip-clop
sound gives it its name, meaning 'Horse of
the Woods' in Gaelic.

Start from the signposted Forestry
Commission car park about 1km from
Kenmore on the minor road turning right
off the A827 just north of Kenmore Bridge.
A wide track leads from the information
boards into the forest: follow the blue and
red waymarker to keep straight ahead
when a path peels off to the right. The
mixed woods are left behind on the ascent
as the larches, spruces and Douglas Firs
favoured by commercial forestry take over.
After a sharp right-hand bend, the track
steepens. At an angled crossroads, a left
turn and then another leads out onto
the rocky outcrop known as Black Rock.
The view over Loch Tay and Kenmore is
spectacular. The reconstructed Iron Age
crannog, with its pointy thatched roof,
perched high above the water on wooden
stilts, can be seen on the far side of the

◄ Kenmore from Black Rock

loch, whilst off the near shore is Priory Island, burial place of the 13th-century Queen Sybilla of Scotland. The viewpoint is bounded by a stone wall, built in the style of the walls around the designed landscape of Taymouth Castle.

Return to the angled crossroads, this time observing the red marker post to simply continue ahead, downhill. There are glimpses of the massive bulk of Taymouth Castle through the trees. Built by the Campbells of Breadalbane, the enormous baronial pile is testament to the wealth of their landowning estates which stretched from Aberfeldy all the way to the west coast. The present building dates largely from the 19th century but stands on the site of the ancient Balloch Castle, built in 1550 for Sir Colin Campbell of Glenorchy. His son, known as Black Duncan, was responsible for the

original planting of Drummond Hill in the early 17th century. Today, the castle stands empty.

A red marker post indicates where to turn right along a sometimes muddy path as it dives back through very densely planted forestry. The trees eventually thin out and, as the path slopes gently uphill, native trees replace the pines with good opportunities for wildlife watching. The path passes above the car park to join the track followed early in the walk. Turn left along this to return.

Chinese Bridge

Drummond Hill

Taymouth Castle

River Tay

golf course

Mains of Taymouth

Black Rock viewpoint

A827

To Killin

hotel

Kenmore

To Aberfeldy

Loch Tay

A827

To Crannog Centre

0   1km

49

Kenmore Hill above Loch Tay

Distance 5km Time **2 hours**
Terrain **waymarked, rough hill paths**
Map **OS Explorer 379** Access **bus (893)**
from Aberfeldy and Killin to Kenmore,
1.5km north of the start (steep climb)

Kenmore Hill has recently been planted
with Scots pine and other native trees to
allow the recovery and expansion of the
remnant Caledonian forest. This
waymarked circuit has superb views over
Loch Tay and the mountains beyond.

The walk starts from the small car park
(SP Woodland Walks), just a short way
south of Kenmore on the slightly hair-
raising Amulree road. It is the longest of
the waymarked trails here and has red
marker posts. From the information
board, branch right uphill. As the path
winds up through the young trees, it gives
great views back to Strath Tay and the
imposing block of Taymouth Castle.

After crossing a small burn, you'll come
to a fork, where you bear right to cross
wooden boards to a stile. Don't cross the
stile; instead keep left towards a gate, but
don't pass through this either. The red
waymarkers lead uphill through an area
where several grand old Scots pines are all
that remain of the ancient Caledonian
forest of mixed pine and broadleaf species
that once blanketed the area. Tree-felling
began in the Iron Age and, more recently,
grazing animals have made regeneration
impossible. However, the landowner,
Bolfracks Estate, has been working with
the Forestry Commission and the local
Countryside Trust to recreate a natural
woodland on Kenmore Hill, including the
planting of native trees and partial fencing
to prevent overgrazing.

The area is home to the black grouse, an
endangered species. If up and about early,
you may be lucky enough to witness their
very distinctive courtship ritual, or lek,
which usually takes place at daybreak

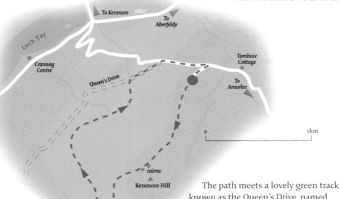

during spring. The males display their fan-shaped black tail feathers to expose the white feathers underneath whilst making a distinctive bubbling call. This exhibition attracts the smaller brown hens who then choose their mate.

The path eventually arrives at a massive cairn near the summit. The highest point is away from the trail over to the left, but this cairn is by far the best viewpoint. Below, almost half the length of Loch Tay can be seen, backed by the towering summits of the Ben Lawers range. Further to the right is the Carn Mairg group of four Munros, while almost directly behind Kenmore is the cone of Schiehallion. From the cairn, carry on along the path to soon cross a stile over a deer fence. Turn left alongside the fence before curving to the right and dropping down through new, densely planted forestry.

The path meets a lovely green track known as the Queen's Drive, named after Queen Victoria who stayed at Taymouth Castle in 1842. (This is also part of the Rob Roy Way.) Turn right for great views over the foot of Loch Tay and Kenmore. From here, the importance of Kenmore's waterside location can be appreciated. Situated on a small peninsula where the River Tay drains the loch, it was created as a model village in the 1760s by the 3rd Earl of Breadalbane, replacing an earlier settlement gathered around a ford. The village celebrates the start of the salmon-fishing season every January with a celebrity-stacked party and, during the summer months, it plays host to loch fishermen and watersport enthusiasts. From this vantage point, it is possible to see boats and canoes darting about like toys. The track finally reaches a large gate and the minor road just beyond. Turn right to climb up the road, reaching the entrance to the car park after about 500m. Another right turn takes you back up the lane to the start.

◀ Summit of Kenmore Hill

Falls of Acharn and the Hermit's Cave

Distance 2km Time 1 hour
Terrain clear paths and tracks, steep climb
Map OS Explorer 378 Access bus (893)
from Aberfeldy and Killin to Kenmore,
postbus (213) to Acharn

This beautiful short walk visits the Falls of Acharn, set in a steep, wooded ravine. Popular with travellers since Victorian times, the falls are approached through a 'Hermit's Cave', which adds to the drama and splendour of the setting.

The village of Acharn was built early in the 19th century to house workers from the neighbouring estates. There is space to park on the west side of the Acharn Burn along the left side of a signposted track for the Falls of Acharn, opposite a beautiful old stone cottage. Follow the sign to walk up the track past the attractive gardens: here, you are on the Rob Roy Way.

A steep climb gives increasingly good views back across Loch Tay to the peaks of Ben Lawers and its nearer neighbour, Meall Greigh. After about 500m, a path peels off to the left and immediately plunges into the entrance to the Hermit's Cave. This artificial, stone-built cave was constructed in the 1760s by the 3rd Earl of Breadalbane to give the most dramatic approach to the falls by concealing them from view until the last moment.
A popular tourist attraction since Victorian times, its visitors have included Robert

◄ Falls in Acharn

Burns, William Wordsworth and his sister Dorothy.

The cave is dark inside, but there is enough light to find your way. In a while, you turn left along a passage that opens out through an archway onto a viewing balcony. This overlooks the highest of the falls in the steep-sided, beech-clad ravine. Retreat into the darkness once more and turn left to leave via the upper exit, returning to the track. Continue uphill, ignoring a sign for a viewing platform to the left which is better reached on the walk back down from the other side of the gorge. A little higher up, the track crosses a stone bridge above the ravine. From the other side, make an immediate left turn to begin the descent: to the right is the onward route of the Rob Roy Way towards Aberfeldy.

Don't miss the detour onto the wooden viewing platforms suspended over the burn to the left. Built by the army in 1989, these give views of the attractive upper falls as well as the weirdly sculpted rocks and potholes of the riverbed. Return from the platform to continue the descent through fine mature woodland. At one point, you can see the Hermit's Cave viewing platform across the ravine, against the backdrop of the Ben Lawers massif. The path leads back down to the village of Acharn, meeting the main road just beyond the phonebox. Turn left to return across the bridge to the start.

Loch Tay

Acharn Point

Acharn

To Kenmore

Allt Mhucaidh

To Killin

Acharn Burn

viewing cave

Falls of Acharn

Rob Roy Way

0   500m

Glen Lyon and Bridge of Balgie

Distance 4.5km **Time** 1 hour 30
Terrain woodland path across steep
slopes, minor road **Map** OS Explorer 378
Access no public transport

**Glen Lyon is renowned for its great
beauty, described by Sir Walter Scott as
the, 'longest, loneliest and loveliest glen
in Scotland'. This walk explores the mid
section of the glen, with fine views as it
climbs through the Ben Meggernie
Birchwood before returning past the
Bridge of Balgie tearoom.**

Glen Lyon is a remote and very long
glen, stretching for 55km from Loch Lyon
at the western end to Fortingall, with its
chocolate-box thatched houses and the
remains of a famous 5000-year-old yew
tree, which is thought to be the oldest
living thing in Europe. Fortingall also
claims, somewhat unbelievably according

to historians, to have been the birthplace
of Pontius Pilate, supposedly the
illegitimate son of a Roman officer who
was stationed here in the last years BC.
Being on the road to nowhere, the glen is
unspoilt and this walk makes an attractive
leg stretcher during any trip into the glen.

The walk starts from the car park at
Innerwick, where there are public toilets,
an information board and leaflets for the
trail. It is worth crossing the bridge over
the Allt a'Mhuic to visit the war memorial
and picturesque Innerwick Church.

A broad path leads into the forestry
from the car park. At the junction, take the
'Upper Route' to Bridge of Balgie. Both
routes have the same total ascent, but this
way is more gradual. The spruces soon
give way to larches and then to beautiful
natural birchwoods as the lower trail
rejoins from the left near a bench.

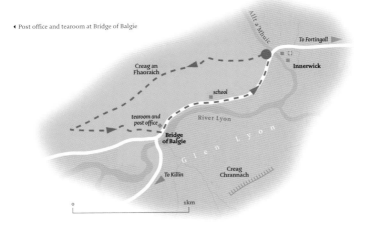

◄ Post office and tearoom at Bridge of Balgie

The path continues to rise to a point where there is a seat with a good view over the floor of the glen. Traditionally, Glen Lyon was home to the Campbells, infamous government supporters and perpetrators of the Glencoe massacre, and the MacGregors, themselves known for being a lawless, landless and outlawed clan. The fertile land in Glen Lyon was the object of cattle-rustling raids by rival clans. In the winter before the Glencoe massacre, a raid by the MacDonalds left the Campbells reliant for food on the mercies of their neighbour, Campbell of Breadalbane, the main instigator of the massacre. 'Mad' Colin Campbell, who built nearby Meggernie Castle in 1585, caught and hung 30 MacDonalds during one of the raids. The castle is a little way up the glen, but it is not open to the public.

The path now gently descends to meet another junction. The left turn provides a direct shortcut to Bridge of Balgie, but to carry on along the main route follow the sign for the viewpoint straight ahead.

There is a seat at the viewpoint – a good vantage point for the mountains enclosing the upper glen. As the path drops once again, the small collection of buildings at Bridge of Balgie and the beautiful white towerhouse beside it come into view. The path emerges next to the post office which also houses an excellent tearoom, open April to October but not on Wednesdays or Thursdays, and there is a craft gallery just beyond. Unless you have arranged a lift, turn left along the narrow road to return to Innerwick.

Ben Lawers Nature Trail

Distance 2km Time 45 mins Terrain clear, waymarked path **Map** OS Explorer 378 **Access** no public transport: nearest bus service is to Killin, 10km away

This short nature trail begins at the car park by the Ben Lawers Visitor Centre, giving easy access to the mid-level slopes of the mountain, home to the most celebrated arctic-alpine flora in Britain. Despite ease of access, this walk can bear the worst effects of bad weather so warm, windproof clothing is recommended.

The walk starts from the Ben Lawers Visitor Centre some way up the minor road to Glen Lyon, off the A827 on the north side of Loch Tay: this steep road is not kept clear of snow and ice, and is sometimes impassable in winter. Ben Lawers is an important ecological site, its lime-rich soils supporting the rarest collection of mountain plants in Britain. Designated a National Nature Reserve, it is jointly managed by the National Trust for Scotland and Scottish Natural Heritage. The nature trail explores a fenced area where the plants are protected from the effects of grazing sheep and deer. Some plants and trees have been reintroduced but most are naturally regenerating.

To begin, follow the surfaced path past the information boards and through a gate. After crossing a boardwalk, go through a gate in the deer fence.

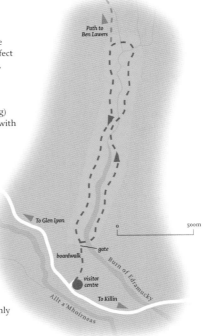

The contrast in vegetation between the two sides highlights the destructive effect of sheep and deer grazing. Once inside, turn right immediately to follow the smaller designated nature trail and cross the footbridge over the burn. The main path (which you return along) is the route to Ben Lawers, often busy with hikers aiming for the summit, passing over the intermediate Munro peak of Beinn Ghlas. Despite its altitude of 1214m, Ben Lawers is relatively easy by hillwalking standards and thus very popular. The National Trust for Scotland has repaired the worst of the resulting erosion through path building and encouraging people to stick to the main routes.

As the nature trail heads up the far side of the Edramucky Burn, look out for the wildflowers – many of them spring flowering – including several varieties of saxifrage. Others, such as the bristle sedge, which can only be found in Britain on Ben Lawers, are harder to spot. The path crosses the attractive stony bed of the burn to the left bank before returning to the right on stepping stones.

On this gradual ascent, the views of Loch Tay unfold far below with a stunning perspective of the surrounding peaks too. The hill to the left is Meall Corranaich with Beinn Ghlas to its right: this conceals Ben Lawers from this side and is often mistaken for it. Looking back across the

road to the right of the visitor centre is the rocky summit of Meall nan Tarmachan.

Further up, you meet the main Ben Lawers path once more, where you turn left and shortly cross the burn. This well-maintained path gives an easy descent towards the car park, rejoining the outward route just before the fence to deliver you back to the start.

◀ On the Nature Trail with Beinn Ghlas on the right

Killin and the old railway

Distance 4km **Time** 2 hours
Terrain clear, flat paths **Map** OS Explorer
378 **Access** buses from Crianlarich,
Lochearnhead and Callander

**Explore the shores of Loch Tay and the
River Dochart on this low-level circuit
from Killin. The walk follows the line of
the old railway to access the head of the
loch for great views across the water and
some beautiful places to picnic.**

Start from the car park on the east side
of Killin. To reach it from the village
centre, take the turning opposite Killin
Outdoor Centre (signed for toilets, parking
and the old railway line) to pass St Fillans
Church. From the car park, join the old
railway line behind the toilets, turning left
to follow the route of the disused track.
This was a branchline that connected the
main Callander to Oban route with Killin
and Loch Tay before it closed in 1939. On

the shore of the loch was a pier, where a
steamer service could be boarded for the
onward journey to Kenmore.

A handsome metal viaduct takes you
over the River Lochay, where you can often
observe canoeists on the water below.
The old railway line now takes you into
pleasant woodland, where you turn right
after 500m and pass through a gate giving
access to the shore.

Loch Tay is Scotland's sixth largest
loch at 24km long and over 150m deep.
The shores were once much more
populated, but the Highland Clearances
and changing economic conditions forced
many to move away. During the Iron Age,
there were a number of crannogs,
dwellings built on stilts or artificial
islands, out in the water. The remains of
one crannog site can just about be made
out near the shore on the left. Now
overgrown with trees and shrubs, it would

◄ The River Dochart

have been part of a thriving community 5000 years ago. There is a reconstructed crannog at the Scottish Crannog Centre near Kenmore at the opposite end of the loch, where you can learn more about these fascinating structures.

Cross the head of the loch passing a number of sandy stretches. Keep following the path as it curves along the shoreline to the mouth of two rivers, the Lochay and the Dochart. Pass by a wooden gate, keeping on the landward side of both the gate and the fence. Avoid an eroded section of riverbank by going through a metal gate a little further on, then continue on the path alongside the River Lochay. Canoeing and fishing are popular pastimes on this section. As it shadows the wide river, the path passes through another small metal gate and crosses a field before eventually returning to the old railway track at a metal gate. Turn left and cross back over the bridge.

Immediately beyond this, turn left down the riverbank, dodging the low-hanging branches which trail with blossom in the spring, to finally pass through another small metal gate. The Lochay can be followed until trees and shrubs block the way, where you turn right to now follow the Dochart upstream.

A farm gate gives access to a field, where the path leads you up a steep bank onto the old railway track. Turn right and shadow this once again to emerge in a small housing estate, where you turn right and look for the continuation of the old railway beyond a turning area. This leads back to the car park at the start.

Map labels: pier, remains of crannog, Loch Tay, River Lochay, To Ben Lawers, old railway line, A827, Killin, To Falls of Dochart, River Dochart, 0 500m

Fingal's Stone and Creag Bhuidhe

Distance 4km **Time** 2 hours **Terrain** very
steep path, can be slippery when wet
Map OS Explorer 378 **Access** buses from
Crianlarich, Lochearnhead, Callander

**This steep ascent of the hill overlooking
Killin offers fabulous views down Loch
Tay. The path passes through an oakwood
and onto open moorland on a rewarding
but strenuous climb.**

Begin the walk from Breadalbane Park
in the centre of Killin. There is parking
next to the McLaren Hall towards the
north end of the village. From here, the
path leads through the park towards the

far left corner. Here, you can detour to
Fingal's Stone which, according to legend,
is the burial place of the mythical Celtic
giant who also gave his name to the cave
on Staffa and the causeway in Northern
Ireland. The story goes that he was
challenged by his love rival Taileachd to
take a giant leap backwards from an
island on nearby Loch Iubhair to the
shore. Fingal failed to reach land and, as
he fell into the water, Taileachd seized his
moment and hacked off the giant's head.
Fingal's body was washed downstream
and found by his followers at the Falls of
Dochart, where they buried it. Taileachd

fled northwards, still in possession of Fingal's head, but was eventually tracked down and killed. Some believe that Fingal gave his name to the town, 'Killin' being derived from the Gaelic *Chil-fhinn*, meaning 'Cell' or 'Church of Fingal'. However, it is also attributed to the more mundane *Cill fionn*, meaning 'White' or 'Fair Church'. After visiting the stone, carry on along the main path through a kissing gate, then head uphill towards the oakwoods.

Go over the stile and follow the path on its steep journey into the trees, before swinging back and emerging onto open moorland. This is a sheep-grazing area and dog owners should keep their dogs on leads during the lambing season from April to mid-June. The path continues to rise steeply, climbing up over a number of grassy knolls before reaching the first crag.

From here, there are great views down over Killin and Loch Tay.

Another two very steep sections follow, where steps have been worn into the slope making the ascent easier. Finally, the top of Sron a'Chlachain, a crag with a small cairn, is gained. This is a fine viewpoint, and many people make this the end point of their walk. However, once you've got this far it is only a relatively short distance to the top of Creag Bhuidhe. The path dips slightly before making the steep, rocky climb, easing off before the broad summit. Here, you'll see three cairns, the largest on the far side of a stone wall marking the true summit at 510m. The views are superb in all directions, taking in many high mountains as well as the loch. The descent is by the same route with the toy town view of Killin getting larger with every step.

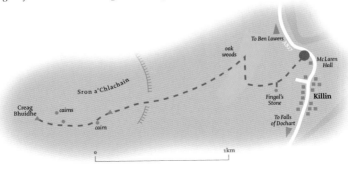

◄ Killin and Loch Tay from Creag Bhuidhe

Falls of Dochart to Acharn Woods

Distance 6km **Time** 2 hours
Terrain forestry tracks, gentle climb
Map OS Explorer 378 **Access** buses from
Crianlarich, Lochearnhead, Callander

**This easy walk follows a section of the old
Killin railway and part of the Rob Roy Way
to explore Acharn Woods, a mix of native
trees and commercial plantations. There
is a gentle climb, with great views of the
Tarmachan Ridge on the return.**

Start from the southwest side of Killin,
where the A827 squeezes the traffic over
the tumbling rapids of the Falls of
Dochart. On the water's edge is St Fillan's
Mill, a reminder of times when Killin was
an important centre for the linen trade.
Flax was grown locally and spun in small
mills like this before being woven into
cloth by an army of home-based weavers.
The mill is now home to the Breadalbane
Folklore Centre. As well as a working water

wheel and industrial history, the centre
houses St Fillan's healing stones, which he
used to cure the sick when he visited and
taught in the area in the 7th century. In
accordance with a long tradition, every
Christmas Eve the stones are given a fresh
bed of straw and reeds from the river.

Follow the main road past a long row of
houses after the Falls of Dochart Inn. Just
before the war memorial, a sign for the
Acharn Circuit points to the left across
the road. (There is some limited parking here,
at the roadside before the bridge and in
the centre of Killin.) Pass between the end
of the terraced bungalows and a newer
house, where the track leads up to a gate
and sign. Beyond the gate, turn right
along the old railway line. This was an
offshoot of the Callander to Oban line
which arrived in Killin in 1886 and was
responsible for the village moving away
from the loch shore. The railway line

◀ Pond in Acharn Woods

actually went as far as the pier on Loch Tay, where a steamer made the onward journey to Kenmore. The railway closed in 1939 and much of the route is now part of a network of footpaths. Follow the old line as it plunges straight through woodland with open fields on the right where deer can sometimes be seen grazing.

This section of the walk is part of the long-distance Rob Roy Way, which follows in the footsteps of the local hero and outlaw. It is also a haven for wildlife, particularly small birds, and flowers. The local primary school has completed a wildlife project here, producing a laminated card which is available along the route. Continue on the railway line, passing the tennis court and buildings at Acharn on the right. The pond in the next field is a good place to watch fish leaping at flies. Soon after this, the track comes to a crossroads. Turn left here and climb gently uphill.

The route now enters an area of forestry, with broom and gorse by the side of the

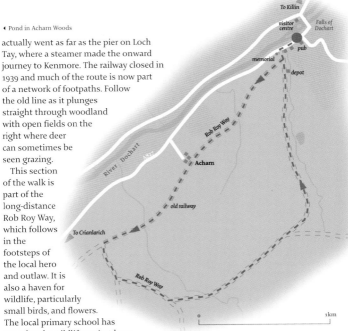

track in places. As you gain height, there are nice views back across Glen Dochart to steep hillsides. Bear left at a junction and left again at the next to join another forestry track.

The route starts to descend with good views of the knobbly Tarmachan Ridge ahead. When you eventually meet a larger track and depot, turn left to follow this downhill to the start.

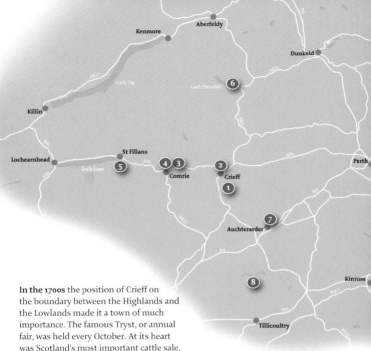

In the 1700s the position of Crieff on the boundary between the Highlands and the Lowlands made it a town of much importance. The famous Tryst, or annual fair, was held every October. At its heart was Scotland's most important cattle sale, to which Highland drovers brought around 30,000 beasts to market from all across the Highlands. The Tryst was eventually moved to Forfar, and by Victorian times Crieff had become a resort town and spa. The great size of the Crieff Hydro Hotel is a testament to its popularity. Built in 1868, it was originally operated on strict religious grounds with a fine of one penny imposed on anyone late for grace at mealtimes. The atmosphere is now more relaxed with many activities on offer. Crieff remains the second largest town in Perthshire.

Today, this area still enjoys a little of the advantages of both the Highlands and Lowlands, with the rich and fertile landscape of Strathearn – complete with the famous golf courses at Gleneagles – merging slowly into the wilder hills to the north and west. Strathearn is packed with small towns and villages, from the 'Lang Toun' of Auchterarder to attractive Comrie on the Highland Boundary Fault, then stretching west to lovely St Fillans on the shores of Loch Earn.

Amulree Church ▶

Crieff and Strathearn

River Earn from Crieff to Muthill

Distance 10km **Time** 3 hours
Terrain good waymarked paths, muddy in
places, minor roads **Map** OS Explorer 368
Access Crieff is well served by buses;
bus (47) from Muthill to return

**This lovely linear walk explores the resort
town of Crieff before following the banks
of the River Earn and a path through
beautiful woodland to Muthill. There is
a bus service back to Crieff.**

Start from James Square in the centre of
Crieff. The town has a colourful past, and
you will be treading in the footsteps of
Rob Roy MacGregor, Bonnie Prince Charlie
and Robert Burns here. Perthshire's
second largest settlement, Crieff grew as a
droving town, with cattle driven from all
over northern Scotland for sale to lowland
buyers at its large trysts (markets). James
Square was laid out in 1731 when the
textile industry began to develop. After
the arrival of the railway in the 1850s, Crieff

became a fashionable spa and resort.

Follow the main street west towards
Comrie, keeping straight ahead on Lodge
Street (SP Stirling) when the Comrie road
branches right. At the attractive square, go
straight ahead onto Drummawhandie
Road and at the T-junction directly across
and down a flight of steps. Turn right on
Sauchie Road, carrying straight on along a
footpath (SP To Ford Road) when the road
bends right. This path runs through
woodland, crosses a minor road at one
point and eventually skirts around the
edge of a cemetery to reach a road. Turn
right here (SP River Earn Walk), passing
several houses and a church. Continue
onto Earnbank Road and follow it to the
busy road to Stirling. Turn right and cross
the River Earn on the stone bridge.

Once across the river, take the second
right onto Alichmore Lane. At a corner,
leave this on the left to join a path signed
for Crosshead. At the kissing gate, climb

◄ Muthill

Map labels:
A85
cemetery
James Square
Crieff
Crieff Bridge
visitor centre
River Earn
flood defence dyke
old railway line
old piers
Bennybeg Pond
A822
Strageath Hall
museum
Muthill

0   1km

uphill keeping the woods to the left. This gate features the first of 'six hands waving at the river', a series of wooden sculptures telling the story of the historical importance of water to Crieff. At the top of the hill, turn left into Thomas' Wood, keeping to this woodland path until an arrow indicates the place to turn sharp left and drop back to the road.

Across the road is the Stuart Crystal Visitor Centre, where in the far corner of the car park a gate on the right leads to the riverside path. This shadows the riverbank at first before diverting, by a marker, onto a small embankment built as a flood defence. Keep close to the fence on the right where a burn divides the land near the river. Climb to a gate and follow the edge of a field before returning over a small bridge to the waterside. Another lovely riverbank stretch meanders to the rusting piers of the former viaduct, where the route of the old railway now takes you along a fence and through two gates before heading under a bridge: this section is often muddy.

At a metal gate, turn left towards Strageath Hall where the driveway steers you round to the right to meet a minor road. Join this to the right for a very short distance before turning left onto a path into Sallyardoch Wood. Keep straight on at a fork and then keep to the yellow markers indicating a right turn through the wood. When the path emerges at a minor road, turn left to enter Muthill. The pretty village centre is well worth exploring, with an old church, museum and hotel. At the main road, the bus stop is on the far side just to the right.

The Hosh and the Knock

Distance **10km** Time **3 hours**
Terrain **paths, tracks and minor roads,
can be muddy in places; one steep
section** Map **OS Explorer 368**
Access **Crieff is well served by buses**

**This figure-of-eight walk climbs the
Knock for a sweeping view of mountain,
moor and strath, as well as exploring the
woods and riverside of the Hosh. You can
also stop off at the Glenturret Whisky
Distillery, home of The Famous Grouse.**

Start from the Knock car park, which sits
high above Crieff and is reached up
Ferntower Road, turning sharp left and
then branching right near the approach to
Crieff Hydro Hotel to carry on uphill. The
route is one of several walks waymarked
by the Perth & Kinross Countryside Trust.
To take in the Hosh loop first, continue
along the road, keeping left at a fork to
pass a high-wire climbing course and go
straight on past the activity centre onto a
rougher track. This gives attractive views
across lower Glen Turret as it descends.

Turn right at a signposted junction to
shortly cross a wooden bridge, bearing left
on the far side and left again at the road.
Soon after Turret Bridge is Glen Turret
Distillery, now better known as The Famous
Grouse Experience. Go left into the visitor
centre car park and behind the buildings to
reach a wooden footbridge over the Turret.

On the other side, a path leads up to a
junction where you turn sharp right and
then left at the next junction (SP Culcrieff)
for a steep climb through the trees. When
you meet a lane, turn left again and, just
before the Crieff Hydro self-catering lodges,
take a signed path on the right. Go straight
across one lane onto the waymarked track
opposite. Now signed for the Crieff Hydro
Hotel, the route soon passes a stone-built
well, dated 1874. The water here was said to
have healing properties and it is what made
Crieff into a fashionable resort, funding the

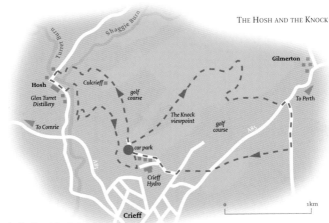

Turret Burn

Shaggie burn

Gilmerton

Hosh

Culcrieff

golf course

Glen Turret Distillery

To Perth

To Comrie

The Knock viewpoint

golf course

A85

car park

Crieff Hydro

0   1km

◄ Lane leading down to the Hosh

Crieff

construction of many of the fine buildings in the town. Sadly, a sign today warns that the water is unfit for human consumption.

As you follow the terrace, you can enjoy fine, sweeping views along Strathearn and over Crieff itself. Join a tarmac lane and, just before a gap in a high wall, with Crieff Hydro ahead, turn left up a steep path signed for the Knock. This accompanies a wall as it climbs the field to reach another set of self-catering houses and the Knock car park just beyond.

To complete the second loop of this route, cross the road and tackle the Knock by the path leaving the other side of the parking area. This soon emerges from the trees at the summit, with views to Ben Vorlich and Stuc a'Chroin.

From the top, a broad, grassy track keeps to the spine of the hill before waymarkers direct you down to a forestry track: bear right onto this. As the track swings round the forested slopes on the far side of the

Knock, you'll see the millennium cairn. Beyond this, immediately turn left onto a track and then left again onto a footpath to almost double back. The path runs alongside the golf course to a gate and track, part of a road built by General Wade. Go straight over this onto the track which leads to the A85. Cross the road with care, following it to the left briefly before turning right onto a minor road signed for Highlandman Loan.

At the junction after Colony Farm, turn right onto a grassy track, crossing farmland to reach a wood of beech, oak and birch. Soon, you cross the A85 again, where the path skirts just left of the golf course and right of the clubhouse. Where it meets a track, turn left to reach the end of Ferntower Road, then turn right for the climb towards Crieff Hydro, taking the road on the right before you reach the hotel. A footpath on the right-hand side leads back to the car park.

Comrie Croft Nature Trail

Distance 3.5km **Time** 1 hour 30
Terrain rough paths, farm tracks, muddy
in places **Map** OS Explorer 368 **Access** bus
(15) between Crieff and Comrie, alight at
Comrie Croft driveway

**This short, varied walk explores the fields,
woods and lochans above Comrie Croft,
with views out across Strathearn and
plenty of wildlife. The route is good for
families who don't mind rough paths.**

Start from Comrie Croft Hostel and
campsite, which is signed from the A85
between Crieff and Comrie. Walkers are
welcome to park at the hostel, and can use
the toilets and buy refreshments during
opening hours. Some parts of the trail may
be used for mountain biking, so care is
needed. A map of the trails can be found
in the car park; stones daubed with purple
paint mark the paths.

Follow the track uphill between the
reception building and the main hostel,

bearing left onto a marked path through
the woods. This little rise marks the
Highland Boundary Fault which separates
the Highlands from Lowland Scotland.
The fault was formed by a massive
collision between tectonic plates
approximately 400 to 500 million years
ago. North of the fault is metamorphic
rock and a more mountainous landscape,
and to the south and east the land lies on
softer sandstone and sedimentary rocks.
The fault has been the source of
numerous small earthquakes in the area.
Early seismic monitoring equipment
dating from the 19th century can be seen
at the Earthquake House on the south side
of Comrie: it's well worth a visit.

Keep left at a fork in the path, then right
onto an uphill track before taking a narrow
signed path to the left, passing a couple of
camping pitches in the trees. On the left, a
dead tree trunk bears the hallmark of
greater spotted woodpeckers: the large

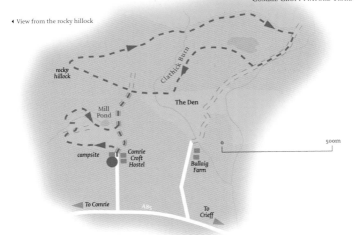

◄ View from the rocky hillock

rocky hillock

Clathick Burn

Mill Pond

The Den

campsite

Comrie Croft Hostel

Ballaig Farm

To Comrie

A85

To Crieff

0   500m

circular holes have been bored by the birds searching for food.

Cross a small wooden bridge to climb through the woods on a faint path. Keep right at a junction, crossing a burn by stepping stones and passing beneath an old mill pond. Braincroft Farm once had its own watermill: the pond was used to store water which, when released, would power the wheel and grind corn. Turn left when you reach the track and pass through double farm gates onto grazing land.

Halfway up the slope, look for a large sycamore tree to the left and follow a vague path over to it. The path then curves around the back of a rocky hillock, giving easy access to the top for great views out over the strath below. After keeping close to the fence, the route heads diagonally across the next field to reach a gate in front of some firs. Go through the gate, using the stones to cross the Clathick Burn and take the faint, rising path to the left on the other side. Soon you'll come to a picnic bench with views over Braincroft Loch and Upper Strathearn. Ospreys, red kites and buzzards can sometimes be seen circling above. When the path meets a junction, turn right to head downhill.

Beyond a small gathering of Douglas Firs, turn right through a gate, keeping just left of the fence around the lochan. Just before you arrive back at the Clathick Burn, turn left to descend via the purple-marked stones. A fence accompanies you down to a stone wall, where you turn right and climb a stile into the Den. It's an immediate right turn in the wood, crossing the burn on stepping stones before emerging onto a farm track. Turn left and left again at the junction to reach the start.

Comrie and the Deil's Cauldron

Distance 7.5km **Time** 3 hours
Terrain path, minor road, avoidable
steep section **Map** OS Explorer 368
Access bus (15) from Crieff

**This excellent circular walk visits the
Deil's Cauldron, a tree-clad amphitheatre
where the River Lednock cascades down a
rocky gorge – with an optional climb to
the Melville Monument above Comrie.**

Start from the car park between the two
right-angled bends on the main road in
Comrie (heading towards St Fillans). Most
of the route is signposted as the Glen
Lednock Circular Walk. From the car park,
turn right along the main road, walking
straight on at the sharp bend to follow the
minor road towards Glen Lednock. Where
the road bends left, leave it to go through
an old stone gateway onto a signed path:
this meanders through beautiful beech
woodland, close to the River Lednock.

To view the first feature on this walk,
the Little Cauldron, a smaller path takes
you down some steps on the right where
you can see the river cascade down a low
rocky gully into a deep pool, before
looping back to the main route. This now
climbs high above the water as it draws
near to the road: stay on the path.

As the sides of the glen steepen, the trail
soon crosses a wooden walkway with the
drops fenced off. At the far end, a flight of
steps leads you down to the viewpoint for
the Deil's (or Devil's) Cauldron itself,
where the River Lednock emerges from a
rock-walled gorge with a double cascade
into a wide pool. The verdant foliage, deep
ravine and crashing water give this spot a
powerful atmosphere. From the Cauldron,
climb the wooden staircase on the right to
the road. As before, bear right to stay on
the pathway alongside rather than on
the road itself.

The visit to Dun More and the Melville
Monument involves a very steep ascent,
and can be bypassed by simply continuing
along the road, rejoining the route further
on. However, the effort is rewarded with
splendid views. A signed path directs you to

◄ Heading into the woods

the left after a short distance. This zigzags unrelentingly uphill at first, easing off for a section before joining a wider track for the final push to the top. The tall obelisk, which can clearly be seen from Comrie, was erected to celebrate the achievements of Henry Dundas, First Viscount Melville who rose though the ranks of the Scottish legal establishment to become Solicitor General in 1766 before turning to politics. He was the last person to be impeached by the House of Lords in 1806 after being accused of improper use of funds during his time in charge of the Admiralty – though he was later acquitted. From the monument are great views southwards to the Ochils, while further right is a glimpse of Loch Earn, with Ben Vorlich and Stuc a'Chroin high above.

From Dun More, return to the track and follow this left. It leaves the woods at a large gate where it joins an old hill track known as the Maam Road. Turn right to pass a wooden seat with a beautiful outlook up Glen Lednock. The descent is made via a series of enjoyable, looping zigzags. When you reach the tarmac road, turn briefly right to find a grassy track (SP Laggan Wood) to the left. This is where you rejoin the main route if the ascent of Dun More has been omitted. At a fork, bear right over a wooden footbridge and take the path downstream to the right.

After climbing a small flight of wooden steps, turn right along a path with dramatic views towards the Melville Monument. Go through a wooden gate and into a dense plantation, ignoring a first minor path to the right to choose the second. This waymarked path wanders through the oakwoods, branching right towards the river and an iron bridge. Turn right to cross the bridge and follow the route of the old railway line behind the main street to the start of the walk.

73

St Fillans view over Loch Earn

Distance **6km** Time **2 hours**
Terrain **track, rough woodland path, road
with pavement** Map **OS Explorer 368**
Access **bus (15) from Crieff**

**A steep climb through the woods above
St Fillans is rewarded with fine views over
Loch Earn to Ben Vorlich, returning
through oakwoods and past the pretty
cottages of St Fillans, beautifully situated
on the shores of the loch.**

This route begins from the Four Seasons
Hotel at the west end of St Fillans, near
two large laybys on either side of the main
road. A lane climbs from the west side of
the hotel, passing the entrance to the
hydro-electric power station. This walk's
objective – the viewpoint – is the site of
the surge shaft where water tumbles into
the ground to drive the turbines in an
underground cavern far below. The lane
passes a couple of houses as it continues

to rise and then doubles back at a sharp
right-hand bend.

Cross the disused railway line by a
bridge and go through an iron gate to
head through birch and conifer woods,
ignoring the gate into the woods at the
next bend (this is used on the return).
Instead, swing left on the rising track,
avoiding another gated track on the right.
Further on, where the track forks, bear
right. Leave the forest at a gate and head
for the flat area ahead. Take the left-hand
fork here for a final, steep ascent to the
fenced-off surge shaft. There are lovely
views along the whole length of Loch Earn
and over to Ben Vorlich, one of the most
popular Munros.

Retrace the outward route as far as the
gate, marked with a yellow arrow, on the
sharp bend in the woods. Go through this
to meander through the pines on a rough,
narrow path. After crossing an area of

◄ Jetty on Loch Earn at St Fillans

open ground with some benches, this re-enters the woods, the pines soon replaced by birches and oaks. Leave the trees at a gate where a track brings you to the right of a pair of cottages and then through a gap in the old railway line. Just beyond the line, turn right through a gate and cross fields and woods behind the new houses.

The path divides just before the village playing field. Keep left and bear left again to go down Shoemaker's Lane to the main road. It is worth making a short detour across the road and pedestrian bridge opposite, bearing right to the village war memorial for the superb views up the loch. Otherwise, continue along the pavement past the Drummond Arms Hotel to eventually return to the laybys and the start of the walk.

Just offshore is Neish Island, once the site of Loch Earn Castle and a bloody episode in the area's history. In the 15th and 16th centuries, the MacNeishes were a clan notorious for cattle and property raiding. At the Battle of Glen Boltachan in 1522, they were routed by the MacNabs and the few survivors retreated to Loch Earn Castle. The clan regrouped and by 1612 had staged an audacious attack on the MacNabs as they returned with supplies from Crieff. The vengeful MacNabs hauled a boat over the mountains from Loch Tay, rowed to the castle and attacked, returning triumphant to Loch Tay with their bounty – including a number of severed heads. Today, the island is a peaceful wildlife haven and nothing remains of the castle.

surge shaft

To Lochearnhead

A85

hotel

St Fillans

Loch Earn

Shoemaker's Lane

To Crieff

A85

hotel

shop

0   500m

Neish Island

memorial

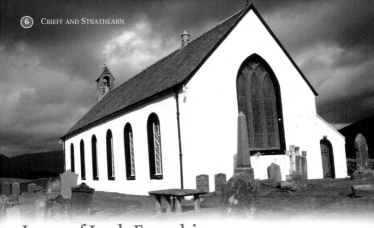

Loop of Loch Freuchie

Distance 12.5km **Time** 3 hours
Terrain track, quiet minor road
Map OS Explorer 379
Access no public transport

Loch Freuchie lies in remote Glen Quaich, with good opportunities to watch birds and enjoy the peace on a longer but straightforward circular hike.

The walk starts from the tiny village of Amulree, where you'll find information about the area inside the church. From the north end of Amulree, where the A822 crosses the River Braan, take the private road signed as a footpath to Kenmore. This soon passes Lochan Cottages and bears left to pass Lochan Lodge, becoming a rougher track as it crosses a cattle grid and heads around the north side of Glen Quaich towards Wester Kinloch Farm.

This route is part of the long-distance Rob Roy Way, which runs for 148km from

Drymen to Pitlochry on paths and tracks used by the outlaw Rob Roy Macgregor in the 17th and 18th centuries. Beyond the farm, the track skirts the north side of Loch Freuchie. Across the water, the Rob Roy Way can be made out coming down the steep-sided cleft of Glen Lochan.

Pass a cottage, a lone Scots pine and another cattle grid to cross open farmland. When the track forks, keep on the lower branch, passing a stone barn. As you climb gently between some drystone dykes, Loch Freuchie comes into view. The remains of a crannog, an artificial island which would have provided a safe house during the Iron Age, can be seen in the loch. According to legend, the island was originally inhabited by a fearsome dragon. As is usual with these stories, a foolish young man named Fraoch followed the request of a lady to gather rowan berries from the island. He managed to complete

◄ Amulree Church

the task and evaded the dragon, but the lady then insisted that nothing would please her except to be presented with the rowan tree itself. Alas, on his return visit, the young lad uprooted his prize only to be ripped limb from limb by the awakened dragon. Needless to say, there is no archaeological or historical evidence to support the story. Although it did not much help Fraoch, rowan trees are still regarded as symbols of good luck.

Continuing on the track and passing through the gates, woodland replaces grazing land. You'll soon see the head of the loch, with good views up Glen Quaich. The farm here has worked to increase the biodiversity of the habitat,

making this a good spot for birdwatching.

The track now passes the ruins of an old settlement, a spot which can be muddy underfoot. After a beautiful old barn on the right, curve down towards Turrerich Farm. Climb the stile, and go through the farmyard and to the left of a bungalow to follow the track round the head of the loch. There is a lovely old stone bridge over the River Quaich before the track reaches the road.

Turn left and follow this minor road all the way back to Amulree, with good views over the water for much of the journey. Although a tiny village today, this was a thriving community prior to the 1800s when land was cleared to make way for sheep. On one single day, 300 crofters left on the same ship bound for Canada. After a three-month voyage they settled in part of Ontario, naming their new townships Amulree and Glenquaich.

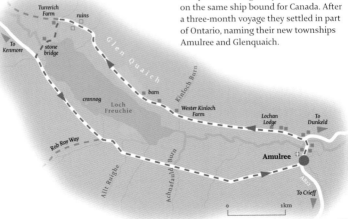

Auchterarder and the Provost's Walk

Distance 7km **Time** 2 hours 30
Terrain paths, tracks, minor roads
Map OS Explorer 368 **Access** buses
from Perth and Crieff; train station
at nearby Gleneagles

**Explore Auchterarder on this easy route
through the centre of town and on the
Provost's Walk, a footpath near the Lochy
Burn and Ruthven Water, with good views
of the Ochils and surrounding farmland.**

Auchterarder is strung out along its long
main street, giving it the nickname of the
Lang Toun. The town was originally an
important centre for the weaving, distilling
and malting industries, before being
sidelined by the growth of Crieff in the
1700s. It became a Royal Burgh in 1200 and
was often host to royalty, generals and
nobility. With the arrival of the railway
in 1848 and the development of the
first golf course soon after,
Auchterarder began to shape
itself into the present-day centre

for golfing holidays. Nearby Gleneagles was
built as a resort by the Caledonian Railway
Company, boasting two 18-hole courses.
The resort now has three championship-
standard courses as well as another of nine
holes, and is owned by drinks giant Diageo.
It will host the 40th Ryder Cup in 2014.
More controversially, the G8 Summit was
held here in 2005 and much of the town
was laid under siege by globalisation
protesters and the opposing army of
security staff and reporters.

Start the walk from outside the tourist
information centre, housed in the post
office in the middle of High Street. (There
is a small car park opposite.) From here,
head southwest up the main street,
passing several independent shops and
the attractive wrought iron sign for
St Kessog's Episcopal Church on the
right. After a short distance, turn
right along Castleton Road to follow
this downhill into farmland. When
you reach the small settlement of

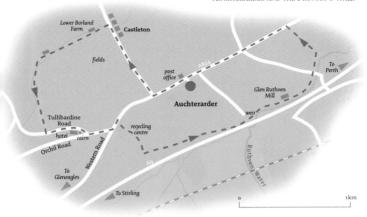

Castleton, turn left along a lane (SP Footpath to Oak Walk) to pass Lower Borland Farm and grazing land.

Continue on the footpath to the left of the lonely house at the end of the track and cross a small bridge and then a stile to enter the oakwood. Head left and follow the winding path up through the trees, going over a small bridge and through a kissing gate on the way. When the path emerges onto Tullibardine Road, turn left to join Orchil Road. A stone cairn sits at the entrance to the Cairn Hotel here, built to commemorate Queen Victoria's jubilee.

Turn left along Orchil Road, crossing Western Road when you reach it and heading left by the park for a short distance. At the corner of the park, turn right onto Quarry Road towards the recycling centre. Just before the entrance, at a corner, a grassy path carries straight on to reach a metal seat. Here, you go left

down some steps and follow this path past fields and close to the busy A9.

Carry straight on, ignoring a path which comes in from the side, to eventually reach new housing. The path continues to the right of the houses, keeping to the trees. After crossing a larger track, follow the narrow path next to the Ruthven Water with its weir and fish ladder. This brings you to a minor road where you go straight on, passing houses on the left.

Directly across a junction, you'll see a lane which leads towards Glen Ruthven Mill, now restored and home to a number of businesses. The path leads past the mill and up a flight of steps to reach more farmland. As it bears left between grazing fields, the path gives great views back to the Ochils before emerging on the main road into Auchterarder. Turn left here and follow the road all the way back to town.

◀ The Old Church Tower

Frandy Reservoirs from Glen Devon

Distance 8.5km **Time** 2 hours 30
Terrain private tarmac road with some
ascent **Map** OS Explorer 386 **Access** bus
from Auchterarder (schooldays and
times only)

The Frandy Reservoirs are set high in the
Ochils on the Gleneagles Estate. This
straightforward walk follows a private
road up the empty glen, with good views
over the water. There is a real feeling of
remoteness here, despite being easily
accessible from nearby Glen Devon.

To reach the start of the walk, leave the
A823 near the head of Glen Devon, just
south of the highest point on the pass,
and take the minor road between blue
iron railings (SP Footpath and The Frandy

Fisheries). There is a parking area on the
left after about 200m. On foot, continue
along the road to head up the glen. You
will soon have good views back down
Glen Devon, with a windfarm perched atop
the smooth slopes of the Ochils.

The road passes a derelict, ornate old
pumphouse, dated 1924, before swinging
left below the grassy dam of the first
reservoir ahead. The Frandy Reservoirs,
also known as the Glendevon Reservoirs,
were constructed by German prisoners of
war during the First World War to supply
water to Dunfermline and Rosyth in Fife.
A wooden footpath sign indicates where a
path branches off to the left. This is part of
the Glen Devon Reservoirs Trail, a new
14km linear walk that runs from here to

the foot of the glen. The route has been created by the Woodland Trust, which has bought extensive tracts of the glen. Some 1.5 million native trees have been planted as part of a scheme to encourage native birch woodland, with the eventual aim of 're-wilding' the glen. The walk continues along the tarmac road, keeping right at the fork to climb to the lower reservoir.

Beyond the dam, the road reaches the Frandy Fishery, where boats can be hired for fly fishing for stocked rainbow and blue trout together with native brown trout. Beyond the fishery, a further climb gives excellent views. The Ochils are bald, steep but rolling hills with slopes of grass and bracken and, as height is gained, the feeling of remoteness increases. This is an excellent area to look out for osprey, buzzards, hen harrier, peregrine falcon, merlin and red kites.

High above a bend in the reservoir, the road reaches its highest point. It now curves left and descends slightly towards the upper reservoir which is revealed ahead. In 2003, the water level fell dramatically and allowed archaeologists brief access to a number of sites including a large bronze age burial mound and the remains of medieval settlements. These are all now back under the normal water level. Continue towards the reservoir, keeping left a fork.

At a further junction, keep right towards the top of the dam; the track off to the left leads to the very remote Backhills Farm. Cross a bridge over the outflow before coming to the dam. From here, you can see the spillway – a curved rectangular basin that appears to suck any overflowing water into the eerie depths below.

The return is by the same route, with fine views towards Glen Devon all the way. This can also be used as the start point for longer expeditions in the Ochils, for which a map and compass would be essential.

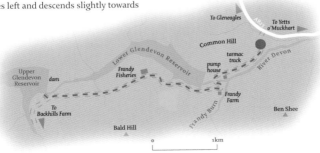

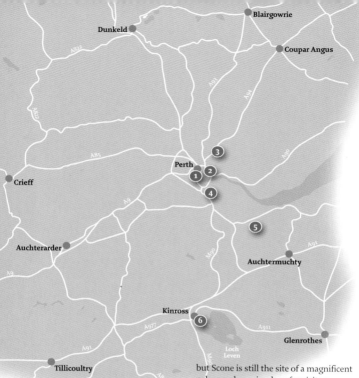

Perth **well deserves its title** as the Fair City. The capital of Perthshire enjoys a splendid location astride the mighty Tay, the country's grandest river. It has scores of fine Georgian buildings, a vibrant range of shops and an array of parks and gardens, including the large, grassy Inches alongside the river. The Kings of Scotland were crowned for centuries at nearby Scone on the famous Stone of Destiny. Today, the stone itself may be in Edinburgh Castle, but Scone is still the site of a magnificent palace and a major draw for visitors.

The area has many gentle hills crowned with monuments and historical remains. These offer excellent objectives for walks, where fascinating local history is matched by extensive views over town and country.

To the south is the town of Kinross, once the seat of a separate county, close to the shores of Loch Leven, the largest loch in the Lowlands. This is an important nature reserve and a fantastic place to visit for birdwatchers.

Perth and the Tay at dusk ▶

Perth and Kinross

A tour of the Fair City

Distance **7km** Time **2 hours**
Terrain **parkland, city streets**
Map **OS Explorer 369 or the free city map
available from the tourist information
centre** Access **Perth is well served by
buses, coaches and trains**

**Explore the historic Fair City and the
beautiful North Inch parkland beside the
Tay, with opportunities to extend the
walk time by calling in at galleries, shops
and museums along the way.**

Begin from the car park on Shore Road at
the north corner of South Inch, part of the
Inches which were traditionally used for
cattle grazing, linen drying and horse
racing. From the entrance, cross Marshall
Place to the Fergusson Gallery. This ornate
circular building, originally a watertower, is
named after Perth's most famous artist,
Scottish colourist John Duncan Fergusson.
Cross to the river, where steps lead up to
the railway and footbridge spanning the
Tay, high above Moncreiffe Island with its
golf course and allotments. On the far side,

turn left for the riverside Sculpture Trail.

After shadowing the Tay, passing fine
works of art, the route reaches Bellwood
Park. Where the path forks, keep right for
Millais' Viewpoint, a carved stone frame
with a view of the Sheriff Court across the
water, then curve left to return to the Tay.
At the next fork, keep left to pass under
Queen's Bridge. Eventually, the riverside
path emerges on Commercial Street,
where you turn left to cross West Bridge
Street and left again to cross Perth Bridge.

Ahead is a statue of Lord Lynedoch and a
thistle monument. The path on the right
of the thistle leads you towards the river,
passing a statue of a soldier and a girl and
the regimental obelisk, then left along the
riverside with great views of beautiful old
houses across the Tay. The path finally
arcs left (a left at the junction) to return on
the far side of the Inches, passing Bell's
Sports Centre and the Black Watch
Museum, housed in Balhousie Castle.

Now join and go left along Rose Terrace,
the Georgian terrace identified by a

◀ The North Inch

prominent rooftop statue of Britannia, which runs parallel to your right. Cross Atholl Street and go left along Atholl Crescent, turning right into North Port for the Fair Maid's House, the oldest secular building in Perth, which was renamed after Walter Scott's popular novel of 1828. Beyond, Curfew Row, once a medieval street of tanners and malters, squeezes between a car park and concert hall to Mill Street, where you turn right.

Cross Scott and South Methven Streets to reach the old city mill where you'll find the tourist information office. Bear right around the far side of the mill where ahead the route goes through a narrow passage beneath the stone tower of Wynd House. When it re-emerges on South Methven Street, take a right and then a left into High Street (pedestrianised further on).

Turn right into King Edward Street and left to St John's Kirk, Perth's oldest building, which dates in part from 1100. From the far side of the church, you'll see the former Central Bank, now a shop. Designed in Renaissance style in 1846, the grandeur reflects the confidence of the bank at the time. Follow St John's Place up the other side of the church, where you'll see a sign for Fleshers Vennel, named after the butchers that once traded in this area. Back on King Edward Street, head left.

Cross South Street onto a walkway and turn left at Canal Street, opposite the faded ostentation of Love's Auction

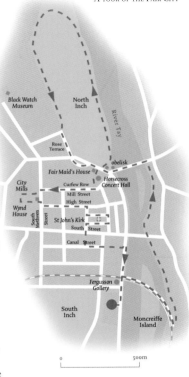

Rooms. This street follows the line of the medieval town wall and ditch. One of Scotland's few walled towns, Perth was an important trading port from the 12th century with a harbour on the river. At Tay Street, go left past the Sheriff Court in order to cross to the river at the traffic lights, bearing right along the water to reach the Fergusson Gallery and the start.

Kinnoull Tower from Perth

Distance 6.5km **Time** 2 hours 30
Terrain roads and paths, steep sections
Map OS Explorer 369 **Access** Perth is well
served by buses, coaches and trains

From the centre of Perth, Kinnoull Hill
gives no hint of the drama of its clifftop
escarpment high above the Tay. The walk
time can be shortened by starting from
the Quarry car park off Corsiehill Road, or
can be combined in spring and summer
with a visit to Branklyn Garden.

Begin the walk from South Inch car park,
just south of the city centre, or simply
turn right from the bottom of the High
Street where it reaches the Tay. Climb the
steps to cross the viaduct/footbridge

opposite the Fergusson Gallery. This gives
good views of Perth along the river.

On the opposite side, go straight ahead
to ascend a flight of steps to the main
Dundee Road. Carefully cross this busy
road, and head right for a short distance
before branching left by the sign for the
National Trust for Scotland's Branklyn
Garden. Originally this, the Barnhill area of
Perth, was dedicated to nurseries growing
soft fruit. Dorothy and John Renton
purchased one orchard here in 1922 and
filled it with plants grown from seed
gathered during early plant-hunting
expeditions to China and the Himalayas.
This small 'haven' is open in summer, but
if you do not wish to visit then turn left
again by the sign for Kinnoull Hill to climb
a steep lane, straight over a crossroads and
past fine buildings. Where the main lane
turns left, head right onto a track and then
left onto a gravel path (SP Kinnoull Hill).
As the route winds steadily uphill, keep
on the main path, turning left at one

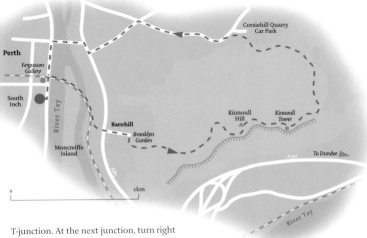

T-junction. At the next junction, turn right via the yellow marker posts.

The summit is a short detour left of the stone table on the escarpment, the superb outlook up the Tay identified on a view indicator. From the stone table, the walk skirts the edge of the escarpment: the high and dangerous cliffs on the right are partly obscured by the trees. Occasional gaps permit dizzying views down to the A90 far below, with the Lomond Hills and Fife beyond. Kinnoull Tower appears, dramatically, on the very edge of the escarpment. Built as a folly in the 18th century, the tower was inspired by the castles along the Rhine in Germany. From here, the escarpment path continues to give expansive views, then swings left to a junction. Keep left here, leaving the escarpment to begin your descent. The marked trail soon rejoins from the left.

At the next major intersection turn left again, signed for the Quarry car park. Yellow markers now lead through the woods, part of the Kinnoull Hill Woodland Park, designated a Site of Special Scientific Interest and providing a habitat for deer and many small mammals and birds. Go over a footbridge to another junction. Turn right to continue downhill by some houses to an open picnic area with good views to the north. Steer left here to reach the entrance to the Quarry car park, turning left down the tarmac road which passes the neo-gothic building of St Mary's Monastery and bends to the right. At the next crossroads, the quickest return is left down the narrow road which emerges by the Isle of Skye Hotel on Dundee Road. It's a right turn, then an immediate left to Queen's Bridge, which you cross to the city centre.

◀ Kinnoull Tower and the Tay

The Scone circular

Distance 9km **Time** 3 hours **Terrain** paths
with one steep moorland section, minor
roads **Map** OS Explorer 369
Access bus (7) from Perth

**This circular walk, created to celebrate the
bicentenary of Scone being moved from
its original position near Scone Palace,
climbs to a folly and the Lynedoch
Obelisk with extensive views, completing
the loop by a wander through woodland,
a golf course and the village itself.**

The village of Scone (pronounced
'skoon') once stood close to the present
position of Scone Palace. In 1805 the
village was relocated, the Old Church
being moved stone by stone
to its new home at the
southern end of the
village. The walk begins

from the car park near this church,
signposted for the David Douglas
Memorial from the main road. Douglas
was responsible for bringing many plants
to Europe from the Americas, including
the Sitka Spruce and the Douglas Fir –
which was named in his honour. He was
born in Scone and started his career as an
apprentice gardener at the palace, but died
in Hawaii, aged 35, after falling into a trap
and being fatally gored by a wild bull.

Passing the church, head along Burnside
to the Scone Arms. Use the crossing to go
over the main Perth Road, and turn left.
After the nursery, turn right into Den Road
to pass houses and a children's play area
on the way into the wooded Den of Scone.
After a wooden bridge, the main path
leads through a lovely area of mature trees
and over a smaller bridge. Keep right as
the pathway rises, turning left onto a
minor road to continue the climb.

Just before the grand gateway to
Bonhard House, turn right along a path
(SP McDuff's Monument). Go through
another gate and woodland before turning
left onto another minor road. Pass the
impressive eagle gateposts at Balcraig,
then turn right for a steep ascent up a

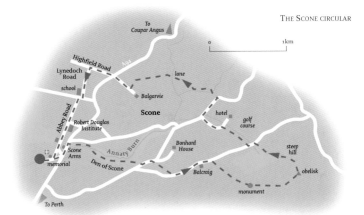

signed path. You pass a covered reservoir before emerging onto moorland. McDuff's Monument, built as a folly in the 1780s, is just beyond, and has great views over Scone and Perth.

An obvious path crosses the moor to the Lynedoch Obelisk, visible on the next hill to the left: keep an eye out for deer and birds of prey on this stretch. A gate by a big tree leads to the obelisk, erected in 1853 in memory of Lord Lynedoch who fought with Wellington to free Portugal and Spain in the 1811 Battle of Barossa: it's a short climb for even more extensive views.

Follow a narrow path to the left down a gully, passing a bench and aiming for the golf course. Cross behind the tee and stick to the clear downhill path to the left, through the trees. When it swings right, carry straight on through the woods on a narrow path. Turn left onto another golf course path, bearing slightly right, before taking a left onto a road. It's then a right down another path just before the large

new houses near the driving range. Bear right to join the main golf course path, dropping down alongside the fairway.

When you reach the driveway to Murrayshall, turn left. At the foot of this, turn right along the road to a clear bend, where you follow a track left through farmland and past the ruins of the Mill of Bonhard. When you come to a road near Balgarvie, turn left and then right towards Scone. Cross the first road and then the main A94 into Highfield Road.

This leads to Lynedoch Road, where you go left and, at the bottom, right and then left into Abbey Road, beside the Robert Douglas Park. Douglas, another Scone man, discovered pectin, the substance that makes jam set, and became a millionaire, leaving much of his fortune to benefit the community when he died. Abbey Road takes you all the way through New Scone, past the Robert Douglas Institute: a right turn at the bottom leads to the car park at the start.

◀ McDuff's Monument

Moncreiffe Hill and the old fort

Distance 8km **Time** 2 hours 30
Terrain waymarked forestry tracks, path
to summit **Map** OS Explorer 369
Access no public transport

**An excellent circular walk explores this
beautiful Woodland Trust site in the
countryside between Perth and Bridge of
Earn. There are grand views over Perth,
the Ochils and Fife from the summit.**

There is limited parking at the start of
this walk. To reach it, take the minor road
heading east from just north of Bridge of
Earn, passing under the M90. After just
over 1.5km, a sign for Moncreiffe Hill
indicates a bumpy track on the left, which
leads to a small parking area just before a
gate. You'll find a map of the walks here.
This route follows the longest waymarked
trail, identified by red markers, which
meanders through the Woodland Trust
site and includes a detour to the hill fort.

Go through the gate and follow the

main track, which rises slightly through
attractive mixed woodland, home to deer
and many species of birds. Ignore the
waymarked route off to the right and carry
on to eventually come close to the noisy
M90. Just when it seems the track might
be bound for the motorway itself, it ends
and the walk continues on the red
waymarked path climbing deeper into the
woods on your right. After looping round
to the right in a clearer area and going
uphill past a small pond, you come to a
junction. Bear left, following the red
marker posts to find a bench on the left at
the very edge of the woods with a good
view towards Perth.

Keep right at the next junction to
continue the ascent through the woods to
another viewpoint bench, this time just
over to the right. At the point where the
red route is joined by yellow waymarkers,
the path turns left to reach the trees at the
foot of a steep grassy dome. This is

◄ Track heading into Moncreiffe Woods

Moredun Top, the true summit of Moncreiffe Hill. The waymarkers keep to the right here, but it is well worth making a detour to the top. Rather than go directly up the steep, eroded path opposite, a better route takes the path to the left of the hill, with a more gradual ascent as it spirals round to the right to eventually reach the summit.

The top is encircled by a grassy bank, which is all that remains of an Iron Age fort. The walls of the fort were made of vitrified stone, rocks heated to such a high temperature that they melted and fused together. How such a high temperature was reached and why it was done are still a mystery to archaeologists. The summit is marked by a small cairn and has terrific views, especially over Perth and the Tay to the north, backed by the first hills of the Highlands. Slightly further round the summit edge is a stone rainwater basin thought to be associated with the fort. From here, the M90 can be seen snaking away south towards the central belt.

Return to the main path and bear left to follow the red waymarkers through the forest, which for this section mainly consists of conifers. Ignore the yellow waymarked route off to the right and keep to the path as it runs along the top of an escarpment for one section, giving great views of the Ochils. Finally, the path curves to the right and drops back to the outward route. Turn left here to return to the gate and the start.

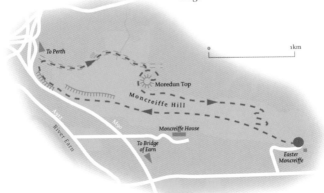

To Perth

Moredun Top

Moncreiffe Hill

0   1km

A 912

River Earn

M90

Moncreiffe House

To Bridge of Earn

Easter Moncreiffe

The Round Tower and Abernethy Glen

**Distance 3.5km Time 1 hour 30
Terrain good paths with steps, minor
road Map OS Explorer 370 Access bus (36)
from Perth**

**Abernethy is a picturesque village on the
very edge of Perthshire and was once
home to Pictish kings. Climb the ancient
round tower in the heart of the village for
great views before taking a short circular
around Abernethy Glen.**

The village is situated on the River Earn
between Bridge of Earn and Newburgh.
For such a small place, Abernethy has a
great deal of history and well repays a
visit. Most noteworthy is the tower, one of
only two remaining Irish Celtic-style

round towers in Scotland, thought to
date from the 11th century. You can
borrow the impressively large key from
the tearoom opposite and climb the spiral
staircase to enjoy the wonderful view from
the top. Be warned, the bell chimes on the
hour and may give you a fright if you
happen to be on the steep ladder beside
it at the time.

Several skeletons have been unearthed
from the building, leading archaeologists
to speculate that it was once used as a
burial place. Attached to the outer wall are
medieval jougs, an iron collar and chain,
remnants of a judicial system in which
corporal punishment was commonplace –
and public. There is also a fragment of a
Pictish stone where, in 1072, Scottish king
Malcolm Canmore was forced to kneel and
pay homage to William the Conqueror.

Abernethy's long history as a religious
centre reaches back to 460AD, with a
monastery created for learning and for
spreading christianity to the Picts. The

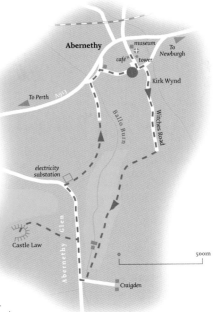

village was later selected as the home of the Pictish kings. Religious power eventually transferred to Dunkeld, though Culdee monks continued to be based here. Most of the church buildings were destroyed during the Reformation of 1560. Abernethy Museum, just past the tearoom, is worth a visit to find out more (seasonal opening).

Cross the main square from the tower, bearing left to then turn right up Kirk Wynd, past cottages and the old church, where the narrow road soon becomes a rough track signed for Witches Road. This is named after a 'coven' of 22 local women who, according to local legend, were burnt to death on Abernethy Hill. Keep climbing, bearing left at a fork. The path (SP Craigden) narrows as it rises by a fence on the right, with good views across the glen to the fort at Castle Law.

Continue through the trees and go down some wooden steps to a bridge over the Ballo Burn. Do not cross this but take the obvious path upstream to reach the minor road at Craigden, where you turn right. When the road starts to drop downhill, it is possible to detour up the path on the left to Castle Law. There is a steep climb to the remains of this hilltop Iron Age fort, but the views are superb.

Leave the roadside when a sign indicates the Rough Glen path to Abernethy on the right. (The narrow hedgerow-flanked path is just past a bench.) It was once a paved route used for transporting coal and lime from Strathmiglo. Eventually, this bears right onto a track where you descend gently to the road into Abernethy. Turn right, passing the corner shop, and follow the road round to the right and then left to the village centre.

◀ Abernethy Round Tower

Loch Leven and Kinross House

Distance 6.5km **Time** 2 hours
Terrain excellent paths and pavement
Map OS Explorer 369 **Access** buses from
Perth and Dunfermline

This easy circuit visits the shores of
Loch Leven, a fantastic spot for
birdwatching, where you can also journey
to an island castle by ferry before
exploring Kinross. The first section as
far as the bird hide is ideal for children
and suitable for buggies.

Loch Leven is Scotland's largest Lowland
loch and an important site for waterfowl,
with the largest concentration of breeding
ducks anywhere in the UK, as well as
attracting thousands of migrating geese
and swans in autumn and winter. This
National Nature Reserve also has the
stunning Lomond Hills for a backdrop.

Start the walk from Kinross Pier, where

there is a café and summer ferry to Kinross
Castle. (Drivers, follow signs for the Castle
and Angling Centre from the centre of
Kinross.) A boardwalk path to the left
circumnavigates the shore of the loch and
passes right through Kirkgate Park, where
you then shadow the boundary wall of
Kinross House. The gardens of this stately
home, built by 'King's architect' William
Bruce in 1685, are famous for their formal
yew hedges, borders and rosebeds and are
a must-see when open in summer.

Just below the stone watchtower is the
castle viewpoint. It is likely that the island
castle seen today is built on the site of a
much older Pictish fort, although no
remains have been found. According to
15th-century records, William Wallace took
part in a daring raid on the castle in 1303.
It later served as a state prison, and Mary
Queen of Scots was imprisoned here for
almost a year in 1567. The viewpoint is also

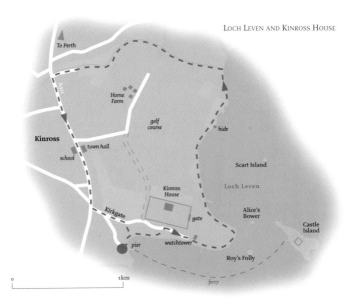

a good spot to watch the overwintering geese, more than 15,000 of which arrive every year: the sight of them flying in at sunset is spectacular.

The path soon passes the elaborate Fish Gate entrance to Kinross House. Above the gate is a carved basket of fish said to contain the seven varieties of fish that could be caught in the loch at that time – salmon, char, grey trout, speckled trout, blackhead, perch and pike. Next, you'll see a right turn to a hide set out over the water amongst the reeds, giving a chance to see whooper swans, teal, reed bunting and even ospreys on Loch Leven.

Return to the main path and take a right to enter woodland. This is a sensitive habitat and dog owners are asked to keep dogs on a short lead to avoid disturbing ground-nesting birds. At a junction, bear left to follow the signed town loop, passing the golf course on the left and heading along a fine avenue of mature oak and beech trees.

Keep on the main path, bearing right through a gap in a stone wall and passing through a wooded area between housing developments. When the path reaches a road turn right and then left onto the main road. This leads all the way back through the centre of Kinross, passing a number of fine buildings including the town hall, which houses the local tourist information centre.

At a sign for Loch Leven, turn left and at the fork keep left again for Kirkgate Park. On reaching the park, bear right to return along the outward route to the pier.

◀ Castle Island from the pier on Loch Leven

Index